TO EAT OR NOT TO EAT

TO EAT OR NOT TO EAT

KAREN MARGOLIS

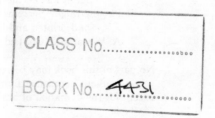
CAMDEN PRESS

Published in 1988 by
Camden Press Ltd
43 Camden Passage, London N1 8EB, England

First published in 1985
in German translation
under the title
Die Knochen zeigen
by Rotbuch Verlag, W. Germany

© Karen Margolis

Designed by Anne Braybon

Set in Baskerville 11/12½pt
by Photosetting & Secretarial Services, Yeovil
and printed and bound by
A. Wheaton & Co. Ltd, Exeter, Devon

British Library Cataloguing in Publication Data
Margolis, Karen, 1952—
To eat or not to eat.
1. Man. Anorexia nervosa
I. Title
616.85′2
ISBN 0-948491-42-6

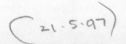

FOR EIA,
ROBIN AND PIERRETTE

CONTENTS

FIRST WORDS

I WAS sobbing, the tears rolling down my cheeks mingling with the apple and flaky pastry that my father was stuffing into my mouth. By his side, a grey-haired psychiatrist was urging him to do it more forcibly. Beside my mother, another psychiatrist was pressing her to support my father more actively. Looking on was my 19-year-old brother, in shock that his sister of 30 should be so humiliated.

It was a fitting climax to the three-year drama of self-starvation in which I had played the leading role, apparently forcing everyone around – especially my family – into the whirlpool of my self-destruction.

But though I declared many times that I wanted to die, and often believed it myself, I never thought it would really happen.

The battle of wills being fought, the drama acted out by those family members and friends willing to participate, was not about life against death. Nor even of me against myself.

I was on hunger strike.

Against my parents: particularly my mother.

Against my twin sister, double threat to my identity.

Against the extended Jewish family that suffocates in the name of love and loyalty.

Against the friends who could not care enough.

Against the system that demands I obey convention.

Against the image I had created to protect myself against the world.

I had chosen to starve to punish all those who tried to suppress my creative instinct – my urge, obsessive since childhood, to express what I experience.

Self-induced emaciation achieves what bitter accusations and

9

angry gestures cannot. The physical presence of a near-skeletal woman shocks everyone around into offering help. It inspires the cheapest and most plentiful of commodities: pity. Even – maybe especially – in an economic crisis, few will begrudge sympathy for those in obvious need. More cynically, most people take some comfort from others' misfortunes and derive some gratification from rendering aid.

So: pity I had in plenty; offers of help by the score. The aura was further enhanced by the label "anorexic", applied readily as soon as my bones became obvious through the thickest garments, and my bizarre eating habits became common knowledge.

Anorexia nervosa is a fashionable disease. Pop stars and princesses suffer from it. Pretty girls, menopausal women and even the odd man share its symptoms. The press and other mass media make much of investigating it.

I believe that anorexia nervosa does not exist. I think it is a concoction of medicine men to explain the mystery of why growing numbers of people – mainly women – are demonstrating their anger by refusing to eat.

I have rejected the label. Not that I am ashamed of it – I have found instead more satisfying ways than starvation to express my fury.

I now refuse once again to accept the pressures imposed on me to conform to the model of women set up by society and enforced by the family.

I have found starvation easier than this honesty.

Now those who rushed to help feel rejected, their kindness spurned. They accuse me of manipulation and insensitivity.

They wanted only for me to get better; yet when I did, they asked why I had changed from the compliant, grateful invalid to the self-assertive individualist. It's only a phase, they whisper (never to my face): she'll soon be back to dependence on us.

The vicious cycle of starvation and remission that is thought characteristic of "anorexia nervosa", seems to me often a self-fulfilling prophecy. You eat because others want you to get better. On gaining weight, your personality returns. They attack it, try to mould it – provoking all the fear and fury that caused you to starve in the first place. They warn of relapse; you comply and stop eating again.

The cures for breaking out of this inexorable round are many and varied. In my experience, most will fail: because they treat the phenomenon not the individual. They substitute patriarchal psychiatrists for patriarchal fathers, both endorsing mothers who would be matriarchs, guarding jealously the feeding role.

In reducing our bodies to bones, we who are labelled anorexic are demanding recognition of our essential selves. I often wished, at less than five stone, that my body would vanish completely.

But this was no suicidal drive. For I never wanted to lose my mind. My hunger strike was rather to protect my thoughts and memories, my most precious possessions.

The category "anorexic" allowed everyone else to ignore my mind, my emotions, my rage and my strong beliefs; to concentrate instead on my vanishing body. The less there was of me, the more they worried. It was such a convenient way to assuage their emotional guilt and confusion.

I write this history as a plea for understanding.

Those who genuinely wish to die will always find a way. Starvation is only one route, and too slow for most would-be suicides. I write for those who want to live but cannot find satisfaction in their lives; who then protest by the hunger strike, one of the oldest forms of political action. It is the favoured weapon of impotent dissidents, of weaponless warriors like the suffragettes.

I write also for all those labelled bad or mad.

I am no longer five stone. I may be crazy. I am almost certainly dangerous. And I am still angry. But I can now express it through my life and my writing.

The tragedy is that many women live their whole lives in the shadow of self-starvation: because they are afraid to be more than shadows of themselves.

1

REDUCTION FROM HISTORY

I SHRANK from myself, shrank from food and love, and, so undernourished, shrank my body until the bones stuck through the flesh.

The victim of my world, I felt hounded for my race, possessed by my past and unwanted in my uneasy presence.

Raised as I was in a Jewish family, under the shadow of the holocaust, images of scapegoats, starving faces and fleshless bones were not unfamiliar. You look like a child out of Belsen, exclaimed my aunt when she visited London from Jerusalem. How could I, who had mercifully escaped the horrors of the previous generation, how could I cast myself in the role of victim?

Do not pity me. Part of me enjoyed it. Only my discontented inner voices kept asking: *why?*

I questioned my history. What had happened to make me want to resist food and pleasure? The many doctors whom I saw made lists of physical illnesses and personal relationships. Ah yes: this type of family, that type of crisis... nothing that made sense. For them, I was not unique: my diagnosed disease, anorexia nervosa, is practically a modern plague. It was easy enough to locate me - or anybody - in the constellation of self-starvers.

Yet a person who denies food and its social consequences must have a strong sense of herself. She is making one of the most powerful statements possible: that she feels her desires and needs are radically different from others'.

The more I refined my body to its basic form, the more urgent became the question: who am I?

I was born in Harare, Zimbabwe, when it was Salisbury, Rhodesia. As a child I lived in South Africa; my family emigrated to England when I was nine, and I was educated in London.

TO EAT OR NOT TO EAT

My father was born in Lithuania; my mother, of Latvian descent, in Cape Town. I have a twin sister, a younger sister and a brother eleven years my junior, who was born in London.

My parents and their families follow the pattern of Jewish professionals: they are hard-working, respected, and on the whole not too conspicuous in public life in the countries they have made their home.

I, too, followed that pattern. I was successful at school; graduated with a mathematics degree from a prestige university. I published my first book at twenty-four and seemed destined for a good career in publishing and journalism.

Throughout my teens and twenties, I cannot recall a time when I recognised depression or sorrow. I suffered the occasional minor heartache over lost love; I always sought to console myself with another lover. I often needed affirmation that my work was acceptable; I usually found it. I was absorbed in politics: friends called me Red Karen and I carried the banners of feminism and socialism with pride.

My family, my self-created image, my identification with causes seemed to protect me. When in need, I had the shield of my twin sister, the most important person in my life. With her I had built my home. I travelled widely; she was always there to come home to.

At times the richness almost overwhelmed me: the pressure to succeed and to enjoy life became too great. My habitual method of breaking the circle was to escape for a brief period to another country. When I could not, I became ill at home.

My first major illness was in 1976. Salpingitis - inflammation of the Fallopian tubes - forced me to stay in bed for six weeks. I felt much physical pain, but there was also pleasure in being cosseted and being left alone in comfort to read and to think. It reminded me of the frequent attacks of tonsillitis I had as a child, when no one scolded me, and I could read as I pleased.

Even after recovery, the atmosphere persisted. Friends knew I was delicate; it was a ready excuse.

In the new year of 1980, my twin took off for California. Just like that. "I'm so happy," she laughed. "I'm going to fly. I'm going to

14

be free. No more work and deadlines. No more family."

No more you, she was saying. After twenty-seven years together, no more midnight twin talks, cuddling together. No more mothering. Never again the warm enfolding that kept the hostile world at bay. She sat on the floor. I lay crying with my head on her lap, and she stroked my hair, saying: "You have to learn to let me go."

On a portrait of her, taken in a photo booth, holding a bunch of flowers that I gave to her, she wrote: Karen - not yet Karen.

She summoned my mother to tell her all the shared secrets that we had never imagined would be revealed. "Don't be angry," she said, pulling me up from the floor where I lay. "Come: dance with me," and she whirled me into the music of *Singing in The Rain*. Then she left.

What is left for me?

What can fill the emptiness?

Food.

I began eating with compulsive frenzy. Or so it seemed. What I actually experienced was the overwhelming desire for food to fill me. My fantasies were far beyond my capacity: I never ate to vomiting, nor even to satiation. It was only in my imagination that I ate until the vast emptiness was filled. But I feared that imagination: for if I ate as much as I wanted, it would be too much, and I would grow fat, I would demonstrate my inability to control myself. I felt lack of control, the possibility of tumbling into a crazy grief.

Help. Somebody help me. An old friend, a psychotherapist, recommended a colleague to me. Three times a week I would lie on the bed in her large light room and complain: I am empty, empty, empty. Nothing will fill me. I have an insatiable desire to eat. "Eat then," said the psychotherapist.

But if I eat, I could never stop: because I will never find the satisfaction that I crave.

To fight the eating compulsion, I took up a dangerous weapon - starvation. It became a way of life that I could not leave.

The first circle was broken when I met accidentally the doctor who had cured my earlier gynaecological problems. She said:

"You are too thin, and your hands are icy to the touch." With a snort for orthodox psychology, she proceeded to diagnose physical causes and to treat them. She succeeded with a wave-energy machine whose powers owe as much to faith as to physical effects.

Supported by the gynaecologist, the psychotherapist and the woman with whom I lived, I emerged again into life, entering a phase of enhanced sociability and creativity. I'm ready to love again, I could say to myself.

On a Christmas trip to Berlin, I met a German man, fell in love, and on impulse abandoned London to live with him.

Living as a stranger in Berlin, I felt free. Carefree. Careless. I became pregnant; and felt for the first time in my life a readiness to give birth and raise a child. My lover could not share that desire. Unwillingly, I had an abortion.

With the loss of my unborn baby returned the loss of my twin. My lover left for Latin America; I felt the loss of him less than that of the child we could have made.

I returned to London, where I found everything the same.

Within months, I returned to the cycle of starvation and fear of food. My twin sister haunted the flat where I lived, where we had lived together. What life could I build here without her?

My parents, friends and family hovered between trying to help and feeling excluded by my determined isolation.

Shivering with a coldness that I could never shake off, I sat at the typewriter composing articles for a medical magazine, giving good advice that I could not follow. Writing, that had always been my solace, became hateful. No pleasure in anything, I complained. I wanted someone to look after me, to resolve at least the basic problems of life: money, keeping warm, passing the endless days and nights.

I did not care for or about myself. I worked continuously, mainly from fear of financial dependence on others, but also to occupy those huge empty spaces of time. How could I have ever wanted more hours in a day, to fulfil my ambitions? What had I wanted to achieve? – I could not recall.

I visited a bevy of doctors. To no effect: I did not want to be cured.

Eventually the strain of running a household became too great. With relief, I left my ghostly flat and returned to the bedroom in my parents' house that I had occupied as a teenager.

For the first time in my life, I retreated into the security of a full-time job, working as a journalist at a weekly magazine.

My output of words increased in inverse proportion to my weight. A shrunken presence in a huge sweater, huddled over a heater, I was a source of wonder to my colleagues.

After work, I returned reluctantly to my parents' house to wait for sleep.

I did not want to be there, in that life; but I had nowhere else to go. Alone, I was lonely. In company, I longed to escape. I did not fear death, though others darkly predicted it. (And sometimes, out of defiance, I would reply that I wanted it: but I never dreamed of killing myself.)

My greatest fear was of other people.

I returned to the psychotherapist, but she could make no contact with me. At last, like everyone else, she begged me to seek medical help. Having proved that she could not help me, I left her forever.

My eyes burned in my hollow face; my legs could carry me only slow, short distances. In the mornings I had temporary blackouts, but always recovered in time to go to work.

I lived for weeks at a time on black coffee and cigarettes.

Perhaps it was the spring that reawakened my desire for life. Perhaps it was a sense that I might see no more springs. I had pared myself to the bone so far that I had nothing further to achieve by that path.

I had pushed my body, my inner self, my outer world of friends and family, to the limits. Only in extremity could I see any future possibility.

I gave up the hunger strike voluntarily, as I had begun it. I sought the help I needed, grabbing it greedily and swiftly. I forced my parents to participate on my own terms.

I had punished myself and my world enough.

Malnutrition emaciates the imagination as well as the body. Physically restored, my fantasies returned, along with my political and social consciousness. The hunger strike is the weapon of an impoverished existence: the world beyond the prison of the starving self offers much richer forms of protest.

2

SUN AND PLANETS

THERE was a time when food and its avoidance seemed the sum of my existence. Much has been written about anorexia nervosa, its counterpart Bulimia (compulsive over-eating) and associated eating problems. I know, because I devoured the literature avidly, searching for a key to unlock my self-imprisonment. I did not find much help from this reading; like everything else, it just confirmed my despair.

When existence dissolves into the dilemma: to eat or not to eat?, you cannot share anything with other people, because sharing involves eating with them. I could not allow anyone else into my cell just as I could not allow food or the contents of books. The descriptions and autobiographical accounts of anorexia usually focus on what it feels like to be in the grip of the malady, and on its dangerous physical effects. What I looked for, and did not find, was why I wanted not only to shrink my body but to lose my personality, my past. Most of all, I craved to know why I hated other people and found them terrifying.

I felt as far away from others as the sun is from the earth. Those around me were distant planets, light years away. To contact them, I had to send out very powerful signals, a constant SOS, otherwise I was in danger of their not being able to see me. Nothing I was, or had achieved, seemed sufficient to make them recognise me, at least in the way I wanted.

The hunger strike is attractive because it focuses others' attention, forces them to react according to the striker's needs and wishes. If you fear people, asking directly for what you want is too difficult. Rejection is unbearable. But even the state that despises and punishes the hunger-striking terrorist is forced to issue bulletins from the prison about his or her health. Anorexics are accused of being similarly manipulative. I do not believe they are any more so than other people; simply that their chosen levers are more effective.

Seeing myself as the sun meant also that I believed, like children do, that the world revolved around me. We are all the centre of our own worlds; but I wanted also to be the centre of other people's, yet without having to involve myself in their lives. By exposing my bones so clearly and dramatically, I could stick out in their minds. I could remind them constantly that I was unhappy.

Life became reduced to a very small constellation compared with the universe of my previous existence. The outside world I experienced only in its direct connection with me, since I knew I could not exert any influence beyond that. I stopped reading newspapers, took no part in current affairs, and rejected all former cultural and political activities.

The immediate constellation became much more significant, and my reaction to it heightened. I felt I was trying to cleanse myself and my life of extraneous matter, trying to reach the internal essence that had become obscured by my image of myself and as others saw me.

Living inside my shell, I did not at the time see how people affected me, nor how I related to them. I complained often that I could not feel deeply myself, and that I felt numb to others. Emptiness, was my description. (Not hunger: I did not know what that meant.)

Strange, since without other people I would not have done what I did. To be sure, I began it without prompting, but I found plenty of encouragement to continue. For the first time in my life, people behaved as I thought I wanted them to. From my solipsistic viewpoint, I could not see that this was because I was behaving as they wished me to: as a reduced personality, adequate but not threatening; in short, like a harmless child.

The hunger striker's cell contains not only the starving victim protester, but also the outside world. If the striker wishes to break out, that world must change, must concede in some way. Help or force-feeding are not concessions, they are imposed solutions.

To give up my strike, I needed once again to see people outside myself, to understand how some force me to play a role I cannot, while others encourage my autonomy at the same time as sharing my feelings. Hunger striking is, after all, an enfeebling process, and there are much better ways to make a political impact which leave you stronger for the next battle.

I emphasise the constellation around me because so many people told me clearly where the blame lay. "Look what you've done to yourself," they said, not seeming to reflect that I did it for them. (The exception was my mother, who firmly believed that I was on strike only against her, to deny her the compliment of good mothering.) The part I played is evident; I want to explore how others acted in my immediate constellation of Family, Friends, Lovers, Medicine Men and Work Colleagues.

3

FAMILY VERRIBLES*
A drama in four acts

The entire action takes place in the kitchen/dining room of a
London suburban house.

Cast of characters
MOTHER
FATHER
FIRST TWIN SISTER
SECOND TWIN SISTER
THIRD SISTER
BABY BROTHER
TWINS' FLATMATE

ACT ONE SCENE ONE 1967

*The family is seated for supper around the dining-table. At the cooker,
Mother is putting the finishing touches to the meal.*

FATHER: I saw an interesting little scene on the way back from
work on my bicycle –

MOTHER: *(Interrupting):* Father, would you come and carve the
chicken?

SECOND TWIN: *(Muttering to First Twin):* Oh, elastic chicken
again. Today, hot; tomorrow, cold with rye bread, chopped
liver and Haimisha cucumbers; and Thursday, chicken soup
with chopped liver and lettuce salad.

FIRST TWIN: *(Also muttering):* Shh... they'll hear you; only
cause another row.

*NOTE: *Verribles* is a Yiddish term for what goes on in families: feuds, arguments,
problems.

FAMILY VERRIBLES

(Mother brings a small plate of meat for Baby Brother; adds some vegetables and ties his bib on.)

MOTHER: I heard that child guidance expert on the radio again – the one who did those tests on The Twins at primary school. She's making quite a name for herself; but I think Tender Loving Care and Commonsense go a lot further than all these psychological studies.

(Father brings over the plate of dismembered fowl.)

MOTHER: First Twin, you're having a wing and some brown meat as usual. Baby brother, if you don't want the mushrooms, just leave them on the edge of your plate; don't keep putting them on Daddy's.

(She heaps First Twin's plate with vegetables, passes it to her.)

MOTHER: Second Twin, you can have your usual leg, and Third Sister can have the other.

THIRD SISTER: I'd rather have the breast, why do I always have to have leg?

MOTHER: You know I like to keep some breast for your father's sandwiches in the morning.

FATHER: Go on, let her have some, I can have salami tomorrow instead.

SECOND TWIN: *(Mutters to First Twin):* It all tastes the same anyway... it's just to prove she can get her way without arguing, 'cause she's the Good Daughter.

FATHER: Anything the matter? Second Twin?

SECOND TWIN: *(Smiles):* No... nothing.

FATHER: Then stop muttering to First Twin. We want one conversation round this table. *(Helps himself to bread.)* Now, I was saying about what I saw on the way home...

MOTHER: *(Helping herself to breast meat):* Well, is it good? Is it up to my usual standard?

FIRST TWIN: The chicken looks a bit odd. There are bubbles in the juice around the meat.

MOTHER: You're not complaining about having chicken again? You know it's so convenient, one bird stretches to lots of meals, and I've got better things to do than slave all day over a hot stove dreaming up gourmet delicacies for you lot. You've no idea what it takes to run a household; remember, a three-year old is a fulltime job, and we don't have a nanny anymore like in South Africa....

FATHER: Hang on a minute, Mother, I think First Twin's right. There is something strange... the oil the chicken was cooked in smells like detergent...

SECOND TWIN: I know what you've done! You mixed up the big cans of oil and washing up liquid... *(Laughs)*... You've cooked a whole chicken and roast potatoes in soapsuds!

(Daughters all laugh. Baby Brother joins in, throwing his spoon across the table. Mother stares at the meat on her plate.)

FATHER: Shut up kids. If your mother's made a mistake, it's because you're so much trouble, you don't let her get on with things.

MOTHER: *(Sighs):* Oh, well, it only confirms what they think already, that I'm a stupid old fool. Maybe we can salvage some of the meat under the skin.

SECOND TWIN: You can't, the skin is porous, it's soaked up the stuff and you'll never get it out. You might as well throw the whole thing away.

FATHER: Don't you tell your mother what to do... you're always telling us what's best. Now Mother, don't worry: we can have chopped liver and cucumbers. And tomorrow I'll take you out for a nice Italian meal; the Sisters can babysit for a few hours.

SECOND TWIN: It's funny really, it reminds me of the time you put bicarbonate of soda in the biscuits instead of self-raising flour... and then you tried to tell us they were meant to be hard as rocks.

FATHER: Second Twin *(That's enough!)* Family meals are not the place for you to entertain yourself by starting arguments. I've had a hard day at work; I don't need to listen to bolshy trade unionists at home as well.

(The family finishes eating; The Sisters all wash up together and go upstairs.)

MOTHER: The Twins are really getting on my nerves, always ganging up on me, and sometimes even getting Third Sister to join in. You don't see it; you're safely behind your desk at work while I'm trying to cope with this madhouse.

FAMILY VERRIBLES

FATHER: It's only a phase, it won't be long before they're grown up and gone, even Baby Brother . . . ; and then you'll probably sit here and tell me you miss them all.

MOTHER: Baby Brother, come here and have a cuddle. You love me even if they don't, don't you?
(She lifts the boy onto her lap and kisses him.)

ACT ONE SCENE TWO 1968

The family is seated for supper around the dining table. At the cooker, Mother is putting the finishing touches to the meal.

FATHER: Today I studied all the statues going up Whitehall on my bike on the way back from work . . .

MOTHER: Father, would you come and carve the chicken?

FIRST TWIN:. *(Sotto voce to Second Twin):* Don't let them see you've got a book on your lap – you know they'll go spare.

SECOND TWIN: *(Also in a whisper):* It's the only way to get through the mealtime boredom, so I don't have to listen to the conversation.

MOTHER: *(Sharply):* OK you two, stop whispering. If you've got anything to say, you can share it with all of us. That's what family meals are for.
(Mother brings a plate of food to Baby Brother; then starts dishing out the rest.)

MOTHER: Now, wing for First Twin, leg for Second Twin; breast meat for me and for Third Sister, leg and some breast meat for Father.
(She addresses Father): Darling, would you like the giblets?

BABY BROTHER: Mummy, Second Twin's reading under the table again.

SECOND TWIN: You little sneak . . . after that nice walk I took you for on the Heath, and the ice-cream you weren't supposed to have, you should be on my side . . .

FATHER: Stop squabbling. Is it true, Second Twin? Have you really got a book on your lap again?

SECOND TWIN: *(Defiantly):* Yes, I didn't want to interrupt my reading for supper, but you always insist I come downstairs, so you

25

can't complain if I bring the book with me.

FATHER: *(Getting angry):* I'm fed up with your cheek. Whose house do you think this is? Have some respect for the work your mother puts into cooking for you.

SECOND TWIN: It doesn't take much work, putting a frozen chicken in the oven and heating up some frozen vegetables. A friend of mine gave me a book about macrobiotic cooking that says soon everyone will die of cancer from the preservatives in frozen food.

MOTHER That's enough of that. You've survived up to now on my cooking, there's no need to throw it back in my face.

FATHER: And I've had enough of hearing the ideas of these *goyim* you insist on hanging around with. Of course they laugh at your family traditions, they have no concept of how Jewish families need to stick together. You listen to me, not to them! I'm warning you, one of these days, one of those people you call your friends will turn round and call you a bloody Jew.

FIRST TWIN: Of course they won't: they're more enlightened than that... anti-semitism's out of fashion in England nowadays.

MOTHER: Don't you leap to her defence. I'm tired of the way you two always stick together against us. Anyway, Second Twin, what is that book you find too fascinating to put down?

SECOND TWIN: It's by a psychiatrist. It's called *Sanity, Madness and the Family* - and the mothers in every case history are a good description of you.

FATHER: Get upstairs before I thrash you! *(Stands up, moves towards her threateningly. She grabs her book and exits rapidly.)*

MOTHER: *(Sighs):* I don't know where we went wrong with that child. She gets glowing school reports, the teachers wouldn't recognise what she's like at home, a completely different person.

FATHER: It's those *goyim* boys she hangs around with, influencing her with the wrong ideas. We never had this trouble when they were still going to the Hebrew youth club.

THIRD SISTER: But Father, it was so boring, the boys just talked about what they got for their Barmitzvahs, and we couldn't join in because girls don't have them.

FATHER: Now don't you start supporting Second Twin; I thought at least you knew better.

FAMILY VERRIBLES

MOTHER: Calm down, everyone. I think there's something else wrong with Second Twin, and I'd like to put a stop to it before it goes further . . . she seems to think books can tell her everything about life, and she's always quoting them against me, as if I don't have better experience than she does. It's typical teenage rebellion, but given she's always been a problem, I think I'll try and get her somehow to a psychiatrist. Not one of the trendy types whose books she reads: someone who understands what mothers of teenage daughters have to suffer.

Now finish up everybody; I want to clear up in time to see the new BBC2 serial that starts at 8.25.

ACT TWO SCENE ONE 1972

(Mother is at the cooker. First Twin, at the table, is sketching Second Twin, who is reading the evening paper. Third Sister is doing her homework; Baby Brother is sitting waiting for his food.)

THIRD SISTER: Honestly, Mother, you'll be late if you don't get ready soon. I said before, we can feed Brother; after all, there's nothing to taking a frozen pizza out of the oven.

MOTHER: That's for me to decide. I like to know he's been properly fed before I go out. It's bad enough I have to leave you lot to babysit; I dread to think what you'll get up to after we've gone. Probably invite boyfriends around.

SECOND TWIN: You would think we were twelve, the way you talk; First Twin and I are at college, after all; and anyway by the time some women reach nearly twenty they've left home ages ago to have kids of their own.

FATHER: *(Entering as she says this):* Well, while you're still in my house, you listen to me and your mother. When you've got your own place you can do what you like. But just remember, it's me who pays your grant for college; without us, you wouldn't be getting this wonderful education that makes you feel so superior. Remember, your mother and I were University students too, once.

Now, Mother, come and get ready or we'll be late.

27

(Exits followed by Mother, who has put the plate of pizza in front of Brother.)

THIRD SISTER: You two are lucky; at least you'll soon be out of here. I'm not going to college in London. Oh, no: I'm applying for a campus university.

SECOND TWIN: Don't worry, we've been thinking desperately of ways to get out. I'm fed up with avoiding the creaking stairs in the dark so they don't know I'm getting back at five in the morning. And they can't be allowed to go on treating us like kids just because they're paying for college. Father only has to make up a share of the grant, he doesn't pay it all anyway; and he doesn't give us the money for books and fares he's supposed to. This summer I'll have to work for money in the library again instead of hitch-hiking round Europe like everyone else at college.

THIRD SISTER: What shall we have for supper when they're gone? How about the frozen beefburgers? We could make cheeseburgers.

BROTHER: *(With mouth full of pizza):* I want cheeseburger too.

THIRD SISTER: OK, I'll make you some if you promise not to tell the parents, you know how they can't stand us eating meat with cheese on.

(Gets up and starts preparing the food.)

FATHER: *(Entering):* What's that in the grill? Funny smell.

THIRD SISTER: Just some beefburgers; we didn't want pizza. I had it yesterday.

FATHER: *(Walking over to grill):* You've got cheese on there! Are you deliberately trying to start trouble, cooking meat and milk together in my house?

THIRD SISTER: I'm only doing it because the burgers are so tasteless without.

FATHER: I don't care about your explanations. This is my house, and as long as you stay here, you stick to my rules. And my rules are: no meat with milk. Get rid of that stuff.

(Younger Sister rises to clear away cooking.)

SECOND TWIN: I don't know what all this fuss is about; you don't stick to the Dietary Laws anyway. There are tins of prawns and mussels in the cupboard, and they're forbidden too. The Laws say, only fish with fins and tails. *(Walks over to the larder.)* Here, I'll show you this jar of mussels, and you show me where the fins and tails are.

FATHER: *(Picking up kitchen knife):* You shut your mouth, girl, or you'll get what's coming to you.

FIRST TWIN: *(Rising):* Father, leave her alone!

(First Twin tries to grab knife from Father.)

FATHER: You let me deal with her: don't interfere. I'm not having such behaviour in my house. Show some respect for your parents.

(He puts knife down. Second Twin moves away to a safe distance.)

SECOND TWIN: I wasn't trying to be disrespectful. I just don't see why there's one law for you and one law for us, and why you won't discuss it rationally.

FATHER: *(Lunging towards her, grabbing her by the throat):* Don't you say another word, or I'll thrash the living daylights out of you!

(Mother comes downstairs, dressed to go out.)

MOTHER: What's all the shouting for? Father, let go of her.

(He does; Second Twin escapes past him into the hall, followed by First Twin, who hugs her comfortingly.)

FIRST TWIN: Okay, we're going out. We're not staying here to be physically assaulted. Look at Second Twin, she's shaking, just like she used to, when she was hiding as a kid and Father used to say he was going to find her and thrash her.

(They put on their coats and go out.)

MOTHER: Well, that's ruined what would have been a lovely evening out.

THIRD SISTER: You can still go, I'll babysit on my own.

MOTHER: How can we? How can we enjoy ourselves after a scene like that? Look at your Father, he's all white. You girls will be the death of him. You always manage to spoil all our pleasure.

(Picks up Brother's empty pizza plate.)

MOTHER: Good boy, finishing it all up. Now do you want yoghourt or chocolate mousse? I suppose I'll have to cook the rest of us some supper now, when I was all set for a night off.

(Sighs as she opens the freezer door.)

TO EAT OR NOT TO EAT

ACT THREE SCENE ONE

Second Twin, Flatmate, Third Sister, Brother and Father are seated at the table. Mother is at the stove, putting the finishing touches to the meal.

MOTHER: Now I know you don't eat meat any more, Second Twin, so I've prepared a special birthday treat – rainbow trout with almonds and parsley; and a cream cake from the bakery round the corner to follow. I couldn't fit 28 candles on the cake, so I thought just one would symbolise things. *(To Flatmate):* You're awfully thin too, though not as bad as Second Twin. Do you also stick to that stupid diet of not eating things for days?

FLATMATE: No, I eat quite a lot; I'm just the thin type.

FATHER: I suppose you've given up trying to persuade Second Twin to eat properly?

FLATMATE: I don't interfere with what she wants to do. Anyway I usually work late, so I don't see much of her till last thing at night.

MOTHER: It's all happened since First Twin left, she was a bit crazy as well. My friend in California wrote that First Twin behaved very strangely when she was there: not at all as she would expect a daughter of mine to be.

SECOND TWIN: Mother, leave off – it is my birthday.

MOTHER: *(Bringing over a plate of fish, potatoes and other vegetables heaped high, and placing it in front of Second Twin):* There, now you eat all that up, Birthday Girl. At least then nobody can say you don't get good nourishing food when you come home to see your Mother.

(She serves the rest of the table.)

SECOND TWIN: I'm writing about sexuality for a weekly magazine.

FATHER: We'll hear about that later, eat your food now. You haven't touched a morsel.

MOTHER: *(Extracting fish bones from her mouth):* Yes, eat up. Look, Flatmate is obviously enjoying it. *(Asks Flatmate):* Do you like my cooking? Yes? Then try to persuade Second Twin to eat the food. I've made it specially for her, she said she would only eat fish. Otherwise we would have had my celebration Birthday Chicken.

THIRD SISTER: I must say, I'm worried too about Second Twin. Friends who know her keep asking me what's wrong with her, as though I'm something to do with it... it's embarrassing, especially after the trouble First Twin caused before she took off for California.

MOTHER: I think she's not eating deliberately to spite me. Come on, try a few almonds, you know how much you like them.... Yes, The Twins have always been a problem, they were too close to each other, it was bound to end in tears. And I always say, if you two had left home in the proper way, instead of rushing off to your college welfare officers and telling lies about how we ill-treated you, just to persuade them to give you a living away grant...

SECOND TWIN: Please, Mother, you're taking away my appetite. I didn't come here on my birthday to be shouted at.

FATHER: Your mother wasn't shouting, she was making a reasonable point. Things haven't been right with you since you left this house. I don't understand why, it must be the life you lead, your friends... we gave you everything you could want or need.

MOTHER: Let's change the subject. Flatmate, did you hear how well Brother did in his exams? He's obviously a chip off his father's block, with his gift for sciences.

THIRD SISTER: *(To Father):* I must tell you later about the economics conference I'm going to in New York. There might be some people there you know.

MOTHER: *(Sighs):* Well, I guess we haven't managed to get Second Twin to eat. You're the one who will suffer, my girl, not us. It's not healthy to be so thin, and when the winter comes...

SECOND TWIN: I can look after myself, you don't have to worry.

FATHER: We wouldn't worry if you had proved you really were grown up, but I don't see any evidence for it.

MOTHER: *(To Flatmate):* I was so proud to have three daughters. Even though I'm a trained professional, I've always felt the most creative thing I ever did was to produce four children. I imagined my daughters would be real friends to me, we'd laugh together and enjoy seeing each other. Instead, they're still causing me trouble at an age where they should have children of their own to worry about, and I should be enjoying the role of grandmother, spoiling my beautiful grandchildren without having to take responsibility for them.

FLATMATE: I don't think the Twins want to have children...

MOTHER: That's just it, they don't know what they want. Now let's all go in the living room and eat the birthday cake. You have to have some of that, Second Twin; otherwise it's not a proper birthday.

(Mother and Father clear the table while everyone else exits.)

FATHER: It's no good carrying on at her, she's determined to prove a point.

MOTHER: Yes, that's true: but she wants to prove it at my expense, to show what a bad mother I am. The rest of the family keep phoning up asking what am I doing about her – as if I ever had any control over her, she's always defied us and gone her own way.

(She takes the tray with the birthday cake and coffee cups into the living room, leaving Father polishing wine glasses in the kitchen.)

ACT FOUR 1982

Father, Second Twin and Brother are seated at the table. At the cooker, Mother is putting the finishing touches to the meal.

FATHER: Today a taxicab narrowly missed me as I was coming back from work on my bike...

MOTHER: Father, would you come and carve the chicken? Second Twin, I suppose as usual you won't be having any... in the five months since you came back to live here, you've only deigned to touch my food about twice.

SECOND TWIN: No, I'll have a boiled egg, I'll make it now.

MOTHER: No, I'll put it on, I don't want anyone else messing around here while I'm preparing the food.

FATHER: *(As he carves):* Well, Second Twin, how's it going at the magazine?

SECOND TWIN: Today the editor offered me a full-time job, but I hate working there, it's such a strain.

MOTHER: *(Snorts):* Of course it is, if you persist in not eating. Don't you know human beings need fuel to keep going, just like cars?

SECOND TWIN: Anyway, I said I would take the job, I need something to fill the time and the money is useful.

FATHER: Well, that's gratitude for you. The editor offers you a job, a good chance, considering the unemployment situation, and you pretend you're taking it under sufferance. I don't understand you... you're so miserable, what would make you really happy? If there was anything I and your mother could do, you know we would. You know how much it hurts me to see you so cold and unhappy and shrunken like this –

MOTHER: Father, the chicken's getting cold, keep carving. Brother has a music rehearsal to get to at half past eight. Here's your boiled egg, Second Twin.

(Father and Mother sit down; Mother dishes out the food and they start eating.)

FATHER: Second Twin, you haven't eaten any of that egg.

SECOND TWIN: Yes, I have had a bit, but it's all runny inside, it makes me feel sick. Do you want it?

MOTHER: Don't take it, Father, don't humour her; she's just playing a stupid game. At her age! *(To Second Twin):* Okay then, starve yourself to death! See if I care!

SECOND TWIN : I don't starve... sometimes I eat too much, you saw me yesterday, a whole packet of peanuts all in one go, and then some cake...

MOTHER: *(Raising her voice):* Shut up! I don't want to hear any more about this food obsession of yours. You eat once in a blue moon, and then complain you're afraid you won't be able to stop. Look at yourself my girl! Who's going to believe that you can't stop eating when you look like a skeleton – a concentration camp victim?

BROTHER: Leave her alone, she's going to cry.

MOTHER: There, I'm not hungry either now. As usual, she's managed to spoil everyone else's enjoyment. Is that what you wanted to achieve? Not content with messing up your own life, you want to ruin ours too? Well, I'm not going to let you. I've done my best, ferried you to doctors, paid for you to see the best specialist about anorexia, and what do you do? Stop going because you say he doesn't take you seriously.

(She starts clearing up the plates.)

Well, I don't take you seriously either, for all your cleverness, your maths degree, your books and articles and famous friends... you're just a silly little girl who's asking to be treated like a child.

(Second Twin exits in tears.)

FATHER: You shouldn't let her upset you so. I'll go up and talk to her.

MOTHER: No, that's just what she wants: special attention from you. Last night you were up in her bedroom for two hours talking with her, till I had to call you down to watch that documentary on TV. And what good did it do? You see how she behaved just now. She can't be like that at work, otherwise they wouldn't have offered her the job; she puts it on just for us, and the more you sympathise, the more you encourage her. I've tried everything: Tender Loving Care, shouting, taking her to doctors... I'm giving up.

FATHER: *(Walking over to kitchen sink):* I can't understand. Where did we go so wrong?

I needed to live at my parents' house, needed the emotional security and the material comforts; needed not to have to take responsibility for looking after myself any longer. So, after a ten-year absence, I returned to the bedroom I had occupied as a teenager.

I continued to work during most of my stay there, so in the outside world I was a professional, an adult. In their house, I could again show my childish moods, though I resented being talked to as a child.

At first they were relieved that I was there, under the parental wing, since I was so obviously physically weak. But as it became clear that nothing would change rapidly, that I was prepared to continue this existence and refused to respond to any cure they attempted, they became weary of me.

FAMILY VERRIBLES

My mother began to show open hostility, especially as family members put pressure on her to do something to help me. From the outside, it seemed the simple solution was to get me into hospital where I could be treated and relieve them all of the problem.

My father, with whom I was always closer, tried hard to help and to understand; but he was caught between me and my mother. My brother, her favourite child, was sympathetic, but wisely opted for living his own, very busy, life at school and with friends.

After a few months, I stopped spending time with my parents, since they mostly watched TV after work, and I was not able to concentrate on it. I spent long hours alone in the bedroom, emerging only to sit with them at meals around the kitchen table. Later, I stopped doing this too.

To complicate matters, my twin sister also returned to live at my parents', after being away in the US and Switzerland for two years. She stayed in the room next to mine, and our relationship alternated between warmth, when she would cosset me and sometimes persuade me to eat; and opposition, when she went off on her own protest, which I found as disturbing as my parents did. At least, I reflected, I was working, whereas she refused to try for a job, asserting that she preferred to be an artist working on her own projects.

In the winter of 1982, I began to have blackouts; once my father picked me up off the floor in the early morning, having heard me fall as he got ready for work. My twin said she could not bear to look at me naked, nor even in nightclothes, because the sight was so pitiful. I began to say that I wanted to die. My mother responded: "How do you think that makes me feel? I, who gave you life?"

My parents suffered. They dreaded inviting friends to the house; they did not want to admit to others that their daughters were not playing the roles expected of such talented, well-educated children. The external image of the happy, model family the parents wanted to project was daily contradicted by reality.

I often asked myself, as my brother prepared to leave home for university, what my parents would do when he was gone, if we were not there. They would have to sell the large family house, which they had mysteriously stuck in since the three daughters left, even though a smaller place would have been easier to manage with only my brother there.

One day in the spring of 1983, my twin sister, after an argument with my mother, told me that my parents were planning to put me in hospital, forcibly if necessary. She said the idea was to get their GP to come and examine me, and immediately to call for an ambulance before I had time to resist.

My brother confirmed her story, saying it was for my own good. I could hear the relief in his voice, he had been having a hard time, too.

"We all love you," he said, "we only want to see you better."

I confronted my parents, who refused to admit to any plan. But from that moment I began to fear what they would do, and determined not to lose the independence I had struggled so hard to keep: the right to run my own life, even if it meant starving almost to death.

Coming back to my room one evening, I had a nightmare vision as I opened the door that my mother was behind it with a knife, waiting to stab me.

I decided that the only way to pre-empt their plots was to take action myself. I arranged carefully for my work at the magazine to be covered; then I asked for time off, and went to visit an old friend from college, now a psychoanalyst. He works at a family therapy centre, and referred me to a colleague there.

This therapist requested that I bring my parents, and any other immediate family members who would come, to the first session with him. It was exactly what I wanted: to find the way out myself, and to get my parents to participate – on my terms – with people whose help I had sought alone.

I am impressed by the techniques used in family therapy to expose and render transparent the relationships that normally go on in the privacy of the home. My parents and brother (and one time, my twin), came with me initially because they wanted to help, they felt somehow connected with and responsible for my plight. In any case, my father and mother have always wanted to participate in solving our problems; the parent role they interpret demands this.

FAMILY VERRIBLES

The family therapy sessions made them uncomfortable. For a start, the therapist was ten years their junior; and he was German. Then, he seemed to practise unorthodox methods. There was the staged family meal in his room, for instance, which generated a major crisis, and after which all the relationships shifted.

He wouldn't be drawn into worrying about my weight or eating habits; seemed to accept that I was at liberty to starve myself. He wouldn't play Big Bad Doctor telling Naughty Little Girl Karen to listen to her Wise Parents. He talked to me as if I were an equal – as if I were the equal of my parents. In the last session they attended, he said he knew of many women like me who played the circular starvation game with their parents for a whole lifetime.

"Karen's strong enough to keep doing it," he said. "The question is," and he turned to look at my parents, each in turn, "the question is: which one of you will break down first?"

4

MEDICINE MEN

CASE NOTES I AUGUST 1980

A young woman calling herself Karen phoned this afternoon. She said a friend had given her the number of Anorexic Anonymous. She described her condition vividly, and obviously has the classical symptoms: cessation of menstruation, long periods of self-starvation followed by occasional bouts of over-eating; inability to concentrate and difficulty sleeping.

She seemed at first suspicious of my Middle European accent, and asked if I was a Freudian. It transpired that she is undergoing psychotherapy with a woman therapist – not a Freudian – and knows something about psychoanalysis. She has also read an article I wrote about anorexia and my curative methods in a scientific journal.

I told her to forget everything she had read; and added that if she agreed to my treatment, she would have to stop seeing her therapist. This is normal medical practice, yet she seemed perturbed by my conditions.

She then began a desperate plea for help, saying that her life had fallen apart since her twin sister suddenly went to America. She complained of emptiness and lassitude, though added that she still works as a freelance writer.

I told her that the twin relationship complicated matters greatly, and that she would need a long period of therapy with me. I warned that her condition could only deteriorate: she would lose her friends and become unable to work. She was briefly defiant, arguing that she had survived up to now and would never forgo her financial independence; then she seemed frightened and rang off. I do not know if she will contact me again; but a firm response seemed the correct one.

PATIENT'S NOTE

I rang Dr. A. because a friend urged me to, saying that he had cured many anorexics. I rang in a desperate moment. He terrified me: sounded forbidding and patriarchal, and as if a cure depended on complete subservience to his will. And who is he, to dictate that I should give up my therapist? (I find her too silent, but at least she hugs me warmly, and doesn't seem to want to judge or to mould me.)

CASE NOTES II DECEMBER 1981

Karen M. came to my surgery near Harley Street with her mother, who was paying the fee so that she could jump the National Health queue. Karen said she didn't agree with private medicine, but her mother insisted; in any case, she has already seen her GP and another doctor, and has given up hope of effective treatment. She only came, she insists, because her parents and friends are so worried she will die that she feels she ought to placate them by seeing an expert.

Her mother, younger-looking than her mid-fifties, is anxious to appear motherly and emphasised her concern. She was quick to tell me that Karen has had the best possible upbringing, and is an accomplished writer; a great puzzle and trial to her loving family.

Karen herself hid inside a large old fur coat, saying it was too cold to remove it. She tried to appear co-operative, and took the prescription for anti-depressants without comment, though she did look apprehensive. She told me she would like to go back to her old life of professional success and political activity, but could find no motivation or enthusiasm for it. I promised her she would in the future be doing a proper job and be back to her old self.

She agreed to attend sessions with me at the Hospital where I run in-patient and out-patient clinics.

TO EAT OR NOT TO EAT

JANUARY 1982

Karen M. arrived for the first consultation looking worse than before Christmas. She said she had abandoned altogether trying to eat, since it caused her distress. I told her this was a temporary phase before eating became normal again; she should try to establish a routine for her days into which eating fitted naturally. She replied this was even harder now, since she was now living in her parents' house with little to occupy her time except a few articles to write.

She threw away the pills I prescribed last time after taking only one, she said they made her feel sick and she was afraid they would increase her appetite (which, indeed, they were designed to do). I weighed her; she was 37 kilos, and I asked if she would agree to be admitted to hospital, where we could control her fear of eating. She seemed terrified, and said she would never allow that to happen.

FEBRUARY 1982

Karen M. continues to resist treatment. Today she came again with her mother. I suggested she come next time alone, and that the visits change from once a fortnight to once a week. She argued that the hospital is a long way from her parents' home, and that she hates bus or underground journeys; indeed, she never goes anywhere except to buy tobacco (she lives mainly on black coffee and cigarettes).

We talked of her twin sister, who has returned to London and is also living at their parents' house. She said she is disturbed by and afraid of the twin who, since her return, seems a stranger. In any case, she asserts, her mother always loved her twin better.

We also talked of sex. She said the thought appals her, though she has had many sexual affairs in the past. She connects this with her unwilling abortion. I said, "There will come a time when you enjoy fucking again." Perhaps it was the deliberate use of the crude word that roused her to anger, the first emotion she has displayed.

She said: "Women are always being told they need a good fuck. It says in the clinical histories of anorexia that it is an attempt to

40

deny maturity and sexuality. That teenage girls starve themselves to retain their childhood, to make themselves thin and beautiful without being sexual."

"Well," she continued: "I was always thin and beautiful; and I'm not a teenager, I'm getting on for thirty, so how do you explain that?"

I was delighted. At last, some life in the pathetic bundled creature. I laughed, and she accused me of not taking her seriously, of treating her like a child.

MARCH 1982

Karen M. continues to complain that she feels worthless, but she has gained a little weight. She says she eats sometimes with her twin sister, who is the only person she trusts; she cannot touch her mother's food. She has been offered good work at a magazine, writing about television, but she denies she is pleased, says she never watches TV and she dreads having to interview people and to write for a demanding editor. "Suppose I have to spend all day in a newsroom? How shall I behave when I can't bear to be with other people? And what if they offer me food?" she pleaded.

I don't take her complaints too seriously, tell her she will manage.

She replies: "That's what people always say. They don't know what it costs."

APRIL 1982

Karen M. says it is becoming more difficult for her to see me, because she is working so much for the magazine. Today, since it is a little warmer, she at last abandoned the dreadful fur coat and thick jumper, and had on a pretty pink sweat-shirt. She said she had to buy it to wear something decent for interviews (hastily, lest I think she was trying to look nice). In any case, she said, yesterday she had overeaten: two chocolate bars and several biscuits in addition to breakfast. Her face had swollen up as a result; which taught her that eating was bad.

"Nonsense," I replied, "today you look very attractive. Your face has filled out." When pressed, however, I did say that overeating could cause face swelling because of water retention. She seemed to want to be treated more as an adult. I told her about the Chinese exhibition I visited recently, with a great ceremonial painted dragon as one of its major features. "You will discover the dragon within yourself," I told her. "What is so bad inside her that she is unable to face?" she wonders.

AUGUST 1982

A letter from Karen M., who has not visited me for over two months. She wrote that she was now working full-time at the magazine, which was on the one hand good because it filled the time and prevented her brooding about food; on the other hand, she had lost more weight, and apart from her work had no contact with others nor wished it. She repeated that she finds people boring and sometimes frightening.

She also said that she had looked up in the library a paper I had written on treatment of anorexia. She noted that though I had cured many patients (that is, restored them to their normal body weight), I observed that many subsequently returned to the former starvation pattern and few ever managed to free themselves entirely from worries about food. She quoted my words back to me with a kind of triumph.

I wrote back saying that she should remember the Chinese dragon whom she would one day discover, and she was always welcome for another appointment.

PATIENT'S NOTE

Dr. B. is an internationally-known expert on anorexia. For my mother it seemed some kind of cachet that her daughter should be treated by such an eminent man; she was also pleased that she had finally persuaded me to admit I was sick, and could tell the family she was taking control to make me better. That is, perhaps, one reason why I resisted his help.

I also found the hospital where he worked a grim and forbidding place. On one of my early visits, I was alone in the waiting room (where the scales he always weighed me on stood waiting too!). A couple of hospital workers entered with a suitcase and began discussing how to dispose of the contents, which belonged to a patient now dead. This confirmed my impression of the bleak Edwardian building as a place one entered and never left; which was why I reacted so badly when Dr. B. suggested hospitalisation.

In any case, I read the advice of Dr. B. and others on how to treat anorexics in hospital. It warned medics that anorexics are notoriously dishonest and scheming, so have to be watched constantly to ensure they do not cheat on the agreed regime. At one time insulin treatment was common; now a system of punishment and reward seemed more prevalent.

Though at times I appeared child-like, I most certainly did not want to be victim of a regime that was worse than any Victorian boarding school nightmare. I was sure, yes, I would lie and cheat just for the pleasure of deceiving the jailers. I treasured most my independence, which is, perhaps, what kept me sane and made me so stubborn for so long. I did not want to yield control of myself to anyone.

I felt that Dr. B. assumed I was like the recalcitrant teenagers who carry dieting too far because they have identity problems, and I felt insulted by that assumption. Perhaps he intended to goad me into anger and therefore back to life; he often seemed to laugh at me or to take my views lightly. This may work with some patients; it had the effect on me of creating further despair that an expert could not help me, coupled with a certain pleasure that I had refused to co-operate and so denied him the satisfaction of another success statistic.

On one of my visits to him, I met an in-patient, a girl in her early twenties from the north of England. She said the hospital was lovely, Dr. B. was wonderful, he had cured her and she was on the path back to normality. She had been forced to give up studying for a social work degree because of her illness. Now she was looking forward to getting a job in a shop.

Would she go back to college? I asked. "Oh, no," she replied, "I could hardly study social work to help other people, when I got in such a mess myself. . . . Well," she concluded, "I must be off to the canteen to have my mid-morning snack. I have to have regular snacks as well as meals, to put on weight in an orderly way."

I shuddered, not only from the cold. Was this the normality, the acceptance of a controlled, reduced existence, that Dr. B. and his fellow specialists were trying to induce in me? It seemed like a lobotomy without surgery; though I am sure the girl who talked to me would prefer her cured existence to the previous hell she had suffered. But I felt there must be another, better way to regain myself.

THE PATIENT'S DIAGNOSIS

In the course of three years I consulted no fewer than seven doctors – six men and one woman. All except the woman diagnosed my disease as anorexia nervosa.

I began the medical round with a visit to my general practitioner, who referred me to experts at a clinic. I never went; I was sceptical of experts. I felt like a buck to be passed on to the nearest specialist. No one wanted to deal with me, the person me: everyone was only too eager to suggest someone else who could help. Once I was safely in the hands of an expert, they could all feel they had done their duty.

To the experts, I was a challenge: another score to notch up when I was restored to normality (that is, to normal weight). Both the doctors whose fictional case notes I have reproduced above are experts in treating anorexia nervosa. I'm not questioning their healing motives: merely demanding what right they have to call themselves experts and to offer the promise of a cure.

I also visited two general practitioners at the group practice my parents attend: a hypnotherapist; and the woman doctor who had formerly helped me with gynaecological problems. Alone of all the doctors, she refused to label me anorexic, and insisted there were physical causes of my malady: food allergies, hormonal imbalances. With this philosophy, she helped me out of the first phase of hunger strike; but after a time during the second phase, I felt her too concerned and motherly, and began to fear her disapproval because I was ignoring her medical instructions. She became part of the circle of my hunger strike, instead of an outside force pulling me away from it. She became a friend rather than a doctor.

When I reflect back on the hunger strike, it is the doctors against whom I feel anger. If family and friends failed to help, they at least could admit to their perplexity and helplessness. Not the doctors. We can cure you, they said. Trust the doctors!

The stories I could tell about Valium and Librium and Ativan and the rest of the pharmacopoeia I received from doctors with reassurances that these pills would help to calm me, would assist in alleviating my fears.

The pills were all the stronger because of my critically low body weight. Once my mother caught me chucking six weeks' worth of Ativan into the dustbin. "They're dangerous," I told her: "addictive." She retorted: "Why do you always know better than the doctors?"

I must have been crazy. Physically weakened, desolate, longing for a way out – an easy way out – of the hunger strike, I went to a new doctor each time that I felt overwhelmed by desperation. I went to the first GP hoping to arrest the symptoms; I went to most of the other doctors under pressure from my parents. Everyone wanted me to get better: going to medicine men was a way to pretend I was trying.

Always there is the latent hope that if you search long enough, you will find someone who really understands, who removes magically all the barriers to recovery. Doctors thrive on that hope.

If the medicine men could be modest and say: "We'll do our best, that's all we can do," I could tolerate that. But they take advantage of our weakness as patients. Like all tyrants and dictators, they tell you they are doing it for your own good.

Six times over, within the space of an initial hour of consultation, a doctor looked across his desk at me and said gravely: I know what is wrong with you. You are suffering from anorexia nervosa. I do not believe in anorexia nervosa. It is a concoction of the medicine men seeking easy explanations for complex and highly individual problems.

TO EAT OR NOT TO EAT

Anorexia is commonplace. People stop eating during phases of their lives for a variety of reasons: a death close to them; the shock of separation from a loved one; loss of job, loss of self-respect, a myriad of other causes. The very reasons, in fact, that make others take to drink or drugs, develop phobias or take off their clothes in public places.

Anorexia nervosa, by contrast, is defined as the specific malady which causes the patient to develop a love-hate relation with food. An extreme relation, that makes food and its rituals become the over-riding force of life. The text-books tell us it was first described in the sixteenth century and has become a marked phenomenon, especially among teenage girls, during the last hundred years. Scores of volumes list its symptoms: loss of menstrual periods; abstinence from food, sometimes alternating with gorging; lack of direction and concentration, frequently accompanied by hyper-activity, including excessive exercising. A combination, in other words, of self-abuse and self-punishment, which the sufferer seems unable to renounce even if she wills it.

All these symptoms occur in many people at some points in their lives. Giving them a name and a treatment to match transfixes the the sufferer in a space from which she cannot escape – without the help of the medicine men.

The label, anorexia nervosa, is a convenient device for doctors and for patients. Once conferred, it is as if patient and doctor have entered into a contract to find a way out together. (In fact, current treatment often involves a contract actually written out, that if the patient co-operates, the doctor will permit rewards.)

I felt relieved, when, by agreeing to see the anorexia expert Dr. B., I had finally accepted that this was the definition of my curious condition. At first it seems shameful and embarrassing to admit that you cannot control your own mind; but then, it happens to so many people, even famous ones . . . And everyone is reassured that the expert has fixed the label on you, it relieves them of the need to find a cure in the dark, you are in safe hands. It also provides others with a reference point from which to view your strange habits and disturbing presence.

To recover, the patient does not need the label. She lives her own misery in her own world; but remember, she chooses that existence. The label is to help the doctors and the rest of society. After all, where would they be without a definition? What could they do without a set of symptoms, a body of knowledge that tells them how the patient behaves and how she is likely to react to a given course of treatment?

The doctor needs the label because, without it, *he would have to start from scratch.*

He would be forced to look at the patient herself, to ask, who is this person? How has she arrived at this point? Not a record of previous ailments, family medical history: no, a real recognition that this is a unique human being; who is, moreover, going to extreme lengths to assert her individuality.

I complained that I was regarded by doctors as a child or as a teenager, since according to their definition, anorexia often manifests itself first in puberty. I am not persuaded that their treatment works for younger women or girls; it certainly didn't work for me.

You might say, but I was clearly demanding to be treated like a child: I had renounced my independence, was living with my parents once again, had shown myself to be needy and greedy as a child is. I would answer: it is not a matter of crime and punishment, of finding the appropriate response to the behaviour exhibited. Saying, you deserve to be treated like a baby, so we'll do just that, simply reinforced my grievance that nobody understood me. They ignored that I was doing an adult job, had almost thirty years of life experience which I could not eradicate, however hard I tried to forget.

I presented symptoms and feelings for the doctors to examine. By and large, they chose to ignore them or to categorise them according to their own preconceptions. Not one doctor said to me, yes, those feelings are real, they exist, let us look at them. Hence, Dr. D. ignored my complaint that over-eating made my face, wrists and ankles swell. I knew it did, I felt it; later I read that this is a common symptom. Several doctors told me to stop reading about the condition, as if to say, such knowledge is dangerous in the minds of impressionable infants.

I believe that the search for knowledge was an important point of contact with the world, that I persisted in maintaining. It was a potential meeting-point with those doctors. They chose to take other paths that led away from me, towards their own prejudices. I can anticipate you, restless reader, asking: But if she knew so much about it, so much more than the doctors, why could she not cure herself?

In any case, I enjoyed my journeys through the corridors (often grimy and paint peeling) of medical authority. It was a game, a challenge, sometimes a satisfying tug of wills. How many failures for medicine could I notch up? How many pounds and ounces could I lose on the way to the next set of medical scales? How many more professionals with a string of letters behind their names could I aim to mystify?

There was another side, too: the self-esteem that comes from being attended to by a doctor, who sets aside time just for you; who concerns himself about your mind and body in a way you cannot demand of anyone else, because it is his job.

But in the end, because it is his job, you feel suspicious, lacking love. How much does he really care? Are you only another statistic? An hour to occupy before lunch in the consultants' canteen?

I admire many doctors for their dedication, but mistrust their power. The power to put a label on the patient, to consign her to the medical machine, even against her will if it is judged she cannot care for herself. Doctors demand the power to make you suspend your own judgement, to abnegate responsibility for yourself.

I was extremely careful not to allow any doctor this power. Though physically weak, I relished the power in myself to resist them. I can say that I might have abandoned my hunger strike earlier had I not received encouragement from my struggle against the doctors.

I was careful to avoid hospitalisation because I knew the loss of power this meant for me. I have heard many women describe their hospital treatment for anorexia. It was required that they become docile, following a strict regime; that they submit to punishment for the crime of denying food. Anorexics are not the only victims of this type of cure: alcoholics, phobics and even cancer patients can be treated as if they are to blame for causing such problems to society and their family. The more it can be shown that the malady is self-inflicted, the harsher the punishment permitted.

Not for me. The very attraction of the hunger strike was that I could be at once independent (keeping my mind intact) and dependent (looking to others to care for my physical needs). I could demand without having to give in return, because I looked so obviously unable to give.

I think the only way for medicine men to break the hunger strike is to put themselves in the patient's empty belly, to ask: "What benefit does she gain from continuing? What would she lose by giving up? And what do I, the Doctor, get out of my relationship with her?"

Anorexia is viewed as a mental problem until its physical effects become too severe. But it may be wrong for doctors to ignore the physical aspects, especially if the patient emphasises them. I was obsessed with forceful feelings about food and its rejection; my body reacted badly when I ate, confirming the danger of eating. No use for others to laugh at it, to say, It's only your fear, a silly fear because food cannot bite you.

I assure you, food can bite with sharp teeth, can threaten to swallow you. Do the doctors know this feeling? I can tell them, it occurs not only in the mind, but in the body, causing nausea as self-disgust rises to the gorge' from the empty stomach.

The only time physical symptoms appear relevant to the medicine men is when they can be used as a threat. The anorexic is warned: Your teeth will decay, your hair will fall out and you will grow a soft down on your body; long-term malnutrition will shorten your life.

I rather liked these dire predictions. Repeated to others, they made my plight seem more dramatic. To me they were abstract since it served my purposes not to be healthy. Towards the end of the hunger strike I began to have early morning blackouts, seemingly caused by a temporary loss of balance. I always managed to pick myself up to go to work in time; I contemplated with something like triumph the achievement of mind over matter that always brought me back to consciousness.

Being in the healing business, doctors hold an interest in enhancing their own position by making the diagnosis seem complex and the cure a miracle of medical science. Around the end of the last century, the fashionable view of anorexia was that it is an endocrine malfunction, something to do with troublesome glands. It was accordingly treated with hormones. The doctors could thus claim that only they could offer a cure.

This approach has gone out of style, to be replaced by a tangled web of semi-Freudian analysis and treatment that assumes rat-like responses in human beings. The philosophy remains that only the experts know how to deal with it.

But it's my body, my mind, I protested inwardly as one doctor after another created me in the image of his own typology. My body feels, albeit unwillingly; my mind reflects, explores, albeit in ever-decreasing circles. Must you become my father and I your child for the cure to take place?

Medical books paint a dismal picture. The self-torturing anorexic will probably never be able to recover a normal attitude to food. She is highly likely to return to starvation and its attendant despair. She is not likely to die, but may be forced to live a restricted existence. The cure, if it happens, may take months or years.

That's hardly an encouragement for the patient. If the treatment is only a short sharp shock, it may be bearable; but if it is to be an unpleasant lifetime, why swap the present cell for a bleaker one? Why bother to forgo the benefits of the hunger strike?

The times when I longed to give up, were the times I tried impulsively another curative avenue. Hence my trip to the hypnotherapist – a dead end, since he could offer me only two years at least of exploration of emptiness. That's also why I went to the first GP; I recognised the recurrence of the old feelings and wanted to arrest them. But by the time the psychiatric clinic offered me an appointment, the impulse was dead.

My sense of time was overwhelming, I felt each slow minute in its passing, yet I felt life itself was passing me by. I waited for something to happen, I knew not what, but I knew it would be a blinding flash, a revelation that would stun me into action. But if a doctor triggers this process, does he not risk showing how easy it is? Does he not risk handing back responsibility and credit for the cure to the patient – for the doctor himself cannot effect the miraculous change, that would take too long. It must come from inside the patient and be exhibited by her.

I knew it was true when wise friends told me I could renounce the hunger strike myself, that only I could do it. But I had to find the right conditions and the right time – and then, the right assistance to keep me to my intention.

I had to learn first that help is a matter of quality. Plenty of help is available for free; plenty more (of an exclusive sort) for large sums of money. The way that society and medicine grades the quality of its help cannot tell the customer whether it will work for her. If doctors can offer anything to the self-starver who wants to taste life again, it must be to show her how to find and to take the type of help she needs.

An Italian psychotherapist friend impressed me recently by describing a patient's problems. "She is so depressed, cannot see any point in living... and she doesn't eat."

"Is she anorexic?" I inquired.

"She doesn't want to eat, that's all," the friend replied.

5

FRIENDS

FAMILIES are the fashionable target for accusation and blame when people show symptoms of psychological distress.

That's probably an advance on blaming the individual alone for her problems: at least it is a recognition that the outside world has some bearing on inner turmoil. I do not believe, however, that the origin of all mental unease lies in some long-buried childhood crisis, entangled solely within family relations.

Friends were as much part of my constellation as was my family. Friends were, in fact, my larger family. As I grew to adulthood, blood relatives naturally became less significant, and friends came to occupy the spaces left by my separation from the family.

The people who told me I was behaving like a child by fasting and other anti-social behaviour were in some respects right. I looked younger than my years, lived rather like a student and refused to settle into a stable job. I was the child that all women are in society before they attain adulthood by marrying and having children themselves.

Without friends, though, I could not have remained like this. No one can forever play a role alone on a stage in an empty theatre. When we describe someone else as acting a part, we must also ask what part we play as supporting cast.

In the circle of guilt and resentment that entrapped me, I often accused myself of dragging my friends into my drama. Some objected that I was trying to manipulate them. But many participated willingly, almost eagerly, showing a positive desire to become involved in my problems.

My friends – the family of my social world – were my first port of call when I felt the beginning of the long unhappiness. I found that the difference between blood and friendship is that friends can always retreat (often using their own blood ties as a reason). When your demands become too pressing, friends can move away from you. Families – at any rate, my family – have a greater interest in trying to find a cure, and so become the last resort.

Within the larger family of my friends, I played another version of the family drama. Wanting to play the child, I always managed to find plenty of people willing to play Mummies and Daddies. In another version of childhood games, we also played Doctors and Nurses, I acting as the patient.

It seems hard to show we care for other people without having to adopt these roles. It is often only in work that peer relations develop clearly; in private life, I do not see many people I know creating roles different for themselves from the Father/Mother/Child pattern.

Accordingly, I narrowed my friend constellation down to those to whom I could admit need and unhappiness; and I avoided social contact with strangers because I could not rely on their accepting me as I wanted to be seen, and taking on their required roles.

Helping roles. Those were the parts that my friends assigned automatically to themselves at the sight of my wasting body and hungering eyes. What can I do to help? they would ask, helplessly. Many gave up when they realised that I was fixed intransigently on the hunger strike. They felt their offers of help rejected, and they did not care enough to hang around to be twice spurned. A few said: I know I can't help, but you know I am always here if you need me; and there were times when I could find some relief in their company for short periods.

And then came the handful of friends who strove to be active helpers, to substitute themselves for the Mummy and Daddy and doctors who were not doing enough to cure me.

Most energetic was Rowan, a red-haired Welsh woman, who was the first to diagnose me openly as anorexic. She was a dear friend of my twin sister who had become closer to me and my flatmate after my twin left for America. Together we commiserated over our shared bereavement; we gave Rowan a key to our flat and she was a frequent and welcome visitor. She always brought food, because she loves to eat. She looks like she loves to eat: she's plump, well-fleshed, and sensitive about being over-weight.

"Eat! Eat!" Rowan would urge, unwrapping a tasty package from a delicatessen. The more she urged, the more pleasure it gave me to refuse.

It was during the first phase of hunger strike, when my flatmate was away in Spain, that Rowan took it upon herself to play nurse in earnest. She would haul me out of my isolation for a drink at the pub, where I would sip tomato juice and talk about food: a harmless substitute for eating. Once she said: "You're anorexic. I looked up books in the library and you have all the symptoms. I've seen it before with my friend Mandy: she went to Tunisia and managed to get her eating down to an orange a day."

I admired Mandy for her self-control. Meanwhile Rowan was proceeding with her determined you-know-you-can-fight-it-if-you-try tone. Mandy got over it... you would never know now that she was anorexic. And if you persist with this starvation, you know what will happen... it's in all the books: collapse, hospital, force-feeding...

Why can't she shut up? I thought.

Guiltily. I knew I should be grateful for her concern, but I wanted her to leave me alone.

One day I came home to my empty flat to find little bowls of food in every possible corner. Nuts, crisps, raisins, cocktail biscuits, pursued me wherever I turned: in the kitchen, in the bedroom, in the living room, even in the toilet. I felt the space I had so painfully created for myself invaded by the nightmare I feared most. Holding the bowls at arms' length, in case the food inside might bite me, I flushed the contents of each down the lavatory.

On my bed lay an article that Rowan had copied from a scientific magazine. It was all about anorexia. I read it avidly. A doctor described the cyclic pattern of starving and gorging; condemned all standard treatments and lauded his own, which I vaguely recall involved psychotherapy and hypnosis. Rowan had done her homework: she had left me his phone number. I rang him, only to be terrified by a German accent predicting doom for me unless I came to see him.

I never went. I could not bear, from that time, to see Rowan either. She was the mother and nurse who would force me to eat against my will.

What kind of friend was she, I asked myself, to terrify me so? I feared her tricks; was afraid of her little bowls of food. She was responding to my playing sick patient. The medical and head doctors were getting nowhere, so what harm was there in Rowan trying her own medicine? After all, that's what friends are for. To stop me destroying myself.

I did not want to play doctors and nurses with Rowan – she knew me too well. She was too close to the reasons why I wanted to starve. Part of me wanted to punish her. I certainly did not want to give her the satisfaction of curing me.

Friends playing doctors and nurses made me feel ever more perverse and self-protective. I did not want them prying into my psychology or inventing miracle cures. I did not want them to define me as anorexic, slapping a label on me. To accept the help of these friends would be to give in, to acknowledge that they were stronger.

I was, however, sending out powerful distress signals. Sometimes they reached more distant planets in my constellation: the old friends who were no longer part of my daily life. There were those who could not resist the signals, who were more attracted to me in my distress than they ever were when I was outwardly a happy, successful person.

I was living at my parents' house when Erika phoned. It was a surprise. She is the wife of an old lover of mine; we met occasionally and with mutual enthusiasm, but had never been close. Erika was worried about me; that, she said, was why she was phoning after so long when we had not seen each other. Why was I at my parents? Was it true, as people said, that I had anorexia?

I recoiled from the word. So that's how old friends were talking about me. I wasn't going to give her anything more to gossip about. "Can't we do anything?" she asked. Her husband's sister and half-sister had both had anorexia, it was something they knew about, maybe they could help with doctors or...

I wished Erika had not phoned. I should have been grateful; instead, I hated her for prying, hated her for making me feel ungrateful. I wished also that she had not phoned because she belonged to a world I wanted to leave, the world that had an image of a Karen I no longer wanted to be. I could not show her my needy self. But then, she would not show me hers. I asked if it was true that she had also been receiving treatment for anorexia. "No, no," she insisted. "I went to the clinic because of insomnia. Yes, I am thinner: but then, I was too fat before... did you hear that I passed my driving test? And my college exams?"

I put down the phone with relief, knowing that Erika would not call again. I had enough to do with professional medical people.

So the patient trap was not too difficult to avoid with friends. The family though... I needed a family. The one I had built with my twin had collapsed. When the hunger strike became a way of life, I found a new family to endorse it, to play supporting cast to my starving role. Each cast member took on her or his part willingly. Each got something for themselves from acting out the drama with me.

As a sister, I adopted Daisy, who worked at the magazine where I wrote about TV. She worked as photographer and general taskperson: an apprentice at the publication owned by her uncle. At twenty, Daisy was still girlish, and very devoted to her family.

All day Daisy would run around doing little tasks for me, bringing cups of coffee, trying to cheer me up, cosseting me like a child, so that you would not guess she was ten years younger. She treated me with the attitude she normally reserved for animals (especially horses), and for babies (notably Prince William).

She liked families, TV family sagas, the Royal family, and best of all, happy families.

Daisy so wanted me to be happy. "Poor little Karen," she would sigh. "Poor little thing. I cry about you at night... try to eat something for my sake. Please, please try..."

When Daisy was sixteen, she was diagnosed as anorexic. Living abroad, she mercifully escaped the normal medical round, and had managed to come out of her hunger strike with the help of her family.

She sought to help, with constant encouragement for me to talk about my feelings. She described how she had overcome her own strike, shared my sense that the feelings were real, sometimes even wept at my despair. She also told me continually how everyone else there admired my work. "If only you would eat, you would be wonderful... ," she would sigh wistfully.

At lunchtime she liked to go out for sandwiches for all the busy writers trapped at their machines and phones. She herself would not often eat in front of others; but she enjoyed talking with me about food, recounting what she had eaten. She felt she ate a lot, and occasionally complained about putting on weight. I had the feeling she wanted others to eat and to get fatter, to make her feel better about her own fascination for food.

Yet I could not eat for Daisy. How she wanted it! I could not do it because she wanted it too much. She still spoke about fatness and food with a touch of obsession: she wanted me to eat to make her feel better about eating. I could not bring myself to fulfil her dreams of a world of happy families. I could not get better for her, though she did make me feel better sometimes when I most needed it. I could not get better for her or for anybody else, not for any friends. I had to get better for myself.

Daisy did not know me before I became a hunger striker. For her, I will always be the anorexic. After leaving the magazine, I met her at a studio opening. I had gained weight; everyone there was saying how well I looked. "How nice to see you again," said Daisy affectionately. "Are you eating?"

There was only one friend for whom I really did try to eat: Nerissa, my mother's cousin. She was distant from the family because she had married a non-Jewish man, an artist; and compared with the other family members of her generation, she led a Bohemian life among artists and actors, a life that had always seemed to me brave, adventurous, even courageous, valuing experience above financial security. When my own friends felt driven away by my isolation, I began to seek the company of Nerissa and her husband. She was family, so would tolerate my strangeness; yet she was also outside the family through her own choice, though it remains the centre of her life. Nerissa likes to cook, with her recipes carefully collected on filing cards, she would produce the most delicious food to awaken my appetite.

It suited her as much as it pleased me to concoct dishes to tempt me out of the hunger strike. It was also a way for both of us to attack my mother, who disliked the fact that I spent so much time at Nerissa's, eating her food when I would not touch anything cooked in my parents' home.

What I had liked about Nerissa as a teenager was that she talked to me like an adult; we had real conversations about things that mattered to us, she was interested in my career and I took seriously her absorption in art.

During the second hunger strike, there was a time when I would go to Nerissa's almost every weekend to be fed and comforted. I would eat: not altogether willingly, but I would eat to please Nerissa, to show I was grateful for her mothering nourishment.

But the more I went to Nerissa to be fed and to get sympathy for my condition, the more she treated me like a child.

At Christmas time I was faced with the prospect of the holiday alone (my flatmate was going away) in a cold flat, cut off without transport. Naturally, Nerissa invited me to stay with them. A chance to feed me properly: our pact was that I would eat three good meals a day, and that I would take the anti-depressants prescribed by the anorexia expert I had just begun visiting.

But then, she became more and more like the mother I did not want, like my own mother. She treated me like a child, scolding me for not eating all the supper. It became harder and harder to eat. I did not want to give her the satisfaction of feeding me, of being her good little girl who ate up all her din-dins. I wanted to have control, if only over whether I ate the Christmas turkey or not. The festive season was hardly festive.

The circle was broken by a tragedy far beyond my control. The day after New Year, I arrived back from a walk, and Nerissa's husband opened the front door to tell me that their only nephew had that morning died suddenly from a brain haemorrhage. They wanted to be alone in their grief. He had telephoned my parents to come and collect me, since it was clear I could not go back alone to my flat.

Shipped through the snow to my family home I felt, not for the first time, an overwhelming sense of nemesis. I brought trouble and death wherever I went. That was the punishment for my hunger striking. That was the punishment for being me; the penalty for the ghoulish game that I was playing with Nerissa.

There was a strange connection. On my walk that day, I had stopped in a graveyard and read the gravestone of someone who had died exactly on my birthdate. I had wished that I was the dead person under that icy earth. Now there was a dead person: and I was forced to go on living.

"Why could it not have been me who died?" I asked my twin sister. She was living with my parents at the time that I was taken there from Nerissa's. It was rather like reliving our adolescence – or living out a second, different, teenage span. We both occupied the rooms that we had lived in as teenagers, at the top of the house, next to each other, isolated from my parents and brother.

In some ways we were more separate than ever before: the separation when she went to America had created fear and guilt in both of us. Yet we found solace in each other's arms, in being together. Sometimes I would eat with her; she never tried to force food down me. Only, she would beg me not to take off my clothes in front of her, she could not bear to see the bones.

What felt terrible was that once we might have been able to help each other, but now we could not.

Besides, we were part of the family again. We took sides. There were times when she sided with my parents, especially my mother. She never used to do that. I didn't trust her as much as I used to . . .

When I started to work at the magazine, the balance changed. Now I was the lucky one, she thought: I had a good job, while no one would pay her to make the art she wanted. But I don't want my job, I cried.

We were drifting apart. Each of our whirlpools was so strong that we could not be sucked back into the other's.

"I'm to blame for your anorexia," she said. "That's what our mother thinks. If I had not gone off to America like that, you would be perfectly okay. But she says we were bound to split apart in that violent way: we were always unhealthily close."

"We're quits," I said. "So you caused my anorexia: well, our mother also said that I was responsible for the nervous breakdown that made you throw up your job and go to America."

I didn't want to fight with her. I wanted her to put her arms around me, to kiss me better, to give me her warmth. But how could she do that without becoming another mother?

"You should get away from your parents' house," the Editor urged. "It's really not good for you to be there, with your twin sister and everything... and you're earning enough now to get a mortgage on a flat."

She talked to me like that occasionally, the Editor, because she thought I needed pep talks to keep going. She cared a lot about me, we were old friends, and now, through her child, she was distantly connected with my family. I could never seem to escape family connections.

The Editor was vigorous and no-nonsense, like an English children's nanny. She said she gave me the job because I was a professional. But if only I would snap out of that awful depression. She was not going to treat me any differently from any other member of staff – neither because I was an old friend, nor because I was anorexic.

She pushed me out to press conferences when I begged to stay in the warm office writing my stories by telephone. She sent me to represent the magazine at this and that industry function. I had to think about what to wear,... what to say... above all, how to avoid food.

The Editor prized reliability above every other quality in her staff. After a year, she told me I could not go on living and working in that state.

Actually, I was beginning to think that I could. At moments I felt a sense of equilibrium, with the job, the routine, the wordless war in my parents' house. I had been doing this for a year, I could carry on. Only, what was the point in living?

"But it's come to the end, when the other staff start worrying about you," the Editor said. "However good you are, I'm not having you disrupting the delicate staff relations at this magazine. If you aren't prepared to change, I'm going to have to let you go."

Where did that sense of equilibrium go? Suddenly I was crying. She was soothing, telling me to go back to the psychotherapist. She said she would give me time off again to go if I wanted to.

She was so kind. Now she was appealing to the old friend, saying how she longed to have the old Karen back again.

But if I started to eat again, I would change, I warned her. I wouldn't be reliable any more: I would be out of control.

I was shaken. I knew then that I could not avoid changing. However disguised, she had delivered the ultimatum. It came at the very moment that I learnt my parents were trying to manoeuvre me into hospital. I had always thought the Editor would protect me from that: now she was saying she would not. For my own good, they were all putting pressure on me, to relieve the pressure of my starving presence on themselves.

What happened when I did eventually change? Everybody changed towards me. I had a new personality, something apart from thinness and aversion to food. I had ideas and opinions. I was very energetic, and for a time, worked even harder.

"I've got the old Karen back," the Editor said, hugging me warmly.

I did not need her to protect or excuse me any longer. Now I was really like the other workers: now I didn't always accept her word or her decisions about our work. I had back the strength to argue. I revived my old trade union spirit.

"You're disruptive," she said. She was really behaving like a lady editor. She was protesting about my being better, because I had become more like me. "You're only doing it to rebel against me," she said.

TO EAT OR NOT TO EAT

My lady editor
Sat on my bed
And said:
Don't treat me like a surrogate mother.

But how can I do otherwise
When she
Treats me
Like a child?

It's the changing that is frightening. Every time you change, you put all your friendships at risk. When I changed into a hunger striker, I alienated many of my former friends. When I changed into another way of life after the hunger strike, I challenged the starving image of myself. Some people found it easier to deal with the needy me than the me greedy for life. If I had been playing doctors and nurses or mummies and daddies with them, they seemed to resent my asking them to play another role.

There were some people who wouldn't join those games yet still remained close, like Belkis, a fellow journalist in my office, who said: "I don't understand why you are working at the magazine. You're wasted. You should be writing novels, creating something."

How could she know? I had a chill of fear, followed by warmth. She thought of me as a person, not a child nor an anorexic: a person with a future. She didn't see me rooted in the thin present.

She is very beautiful, Belkis. Why does she bother with me? I kept thinking. She's so lovely . . . her skin is the smoothest brown, her hands and feet exquisitely petite. She was Indian, born in Uganda. When she talked about her country, I recalled my childhood in South Africa. When she spoke of her Muslim observances, it reminded me of my Jewish upbringing. There were a lot of reasons for us to be friends; but I didn't want to make friends, I wanted to be isolated.

She persisted. At first she mentioned eating, suggested an Indian healer, a hospital nutritionist who might help. When I did not respond, she didn't push it. She did not want to play those games. Why?

FRIENDS

She saw me as a good writer: the respect was mutual. She was less experienced as a journalist but knew much more about the work at the magazine and the background to the TV industry. Sometimes we helped each other. We would meet in a cafe and work together on difficult stories. Sometimes the whole meeting we would not talk about food or starving, we were too intent on the work together.

Belkis made me forget that I was a reduced person. My behaviour and appearance might be lopsided, but she saw something else, the me that might be. She did not know me before the hunger strike, so it is a tribute to her imagination. To Belkis, I was not just an empty shell producing empty words. She also made the work seem more meaningful.

She turned me into a helper, negating my helplessness. I had to defend her against the Editor's criticisms; suddenly she was casting me in a new role, being responsible for her, protecting our friendship.

When I stopped the hunger strike, Belkis did not claim the cure, nor recoil from the eating me. "You're like a spider," she said: "You weave webs with people and dreams."

B. would not be pulled into my web, the tangled web of starvation. Next to my twin sister, she was the woman closest in my life. The three of us had lived together for nine years, ever since we had all left our parents' homes. We were like a family. B. was the quiet one, an only child, at times keeping very much to herself, wanting to be left alone.

I was emerging from the first phase of hunger strike. All night I did not sleep, restlessly waiting for the new day. When it dawned, B. crept into my room. It had been for her also a sleepless night. All night she had been drawing a picture of me.

A pale wraith with a blue-tinged skin, with huge accusing eyes, with lank weeping hair, scrawny limbs, spidery hands and feet. The breastless chest? Was that me?

"That's you," she said. "Starving or not starving, I find you beautiful. Look." She pointed to her drawing. Rising from my crotch to my heart was a roseate flame, pure white at the centre. It had a vulva shape. I stared at it, with fear and joy.

TO EAT OR NOT TO EAT

Before she met me, B. had guarded her own life against her parents, against too much loving of an only child. She guarded her life against me. My hunger strike was not going to disturb her work or her other relationships. She was always warm, friendly, solicitous, but to an equal, not a child or a patient. Sometimes she wanted to be a child or patient too, but she gave up trying to get help from me. She was not angry or disappointed. "That's Karen's karma," she would say.

She wanted me to continue living with her, but when I moved to my parents, she accepted it with some relief. It was I who was disappointed: I had failed to force a reaction from her. I had pushed the friendship as far as it would go.

She would not let go. She came to visit me at the magazine; even came to my parents' house, though she hated the atmosphere there. She ignored the hunger strike, would not comment on my emaciation; she talked of friends and work as if they meant something to her and to me. Sometimes she said I looked bad. "It's not the thinness, it's that sadness in your eyes," she would say. I felt uncomfortable, reminded of all the times together when we had been happy. She did not come to make me feel comfortable: she came to preserve our friendship, whatever I was or would become.

I seemed to need the affirmation that friends cared enough about me to change their own lives, to deny themselves for me. Yet only my parents would respond with the strong reaction I was trying to provoke.

The friends who allowed me to live my crisis were rare. They were usually the ones who could admit to crises themselves. Everyone else seemed to be pretending they were leading something called a normal life. If only I tried I could join them. I looked at them: did I want to live their kinds of life? Would I be happy?

I became more and more open about my distress.

I wanted friends to stop putting pressure on me. My younger sister accused: "Look what you're doing to everyone. Your old friends whom you won't visit come to me almost in tears, asking what is to be done about you. Everyone wants to help. Why won't you let them?"

FRIENDS

There was no point, no reason. Nothing. Not even the spring could thaw my frozen bones. I felt hunted, yet unable to flee. Crowds of concerned faces haunted me. For your own good, for your own good. Crowds of concerned faces, conspiring to make me better against my will.

I worked as late as I could. One night, walking along Oxford Street to the bus stop, I could see no reason to walk any further. I lay down on the pavement in the fluorescent light of a shop window. I was weak, but that's not the reason why I lay down. I lay down because there was nowhere further to go.

"Anything wrong, ducks? Can I help? You OK?" A middle-aged Cockney woman with a headscarf was bending over me.

"Had a funny turn, then? – you're very white," she said, patting my head.

I sat up against the shop window.

"I'm OK. Just a bit dizzy, that's all. OK – really."

She went. I sat there, staring at my feet. The pavement was wet; it was drizzling again. A couple of people stopped curiously, then walked away. I sat; and sat. Several buses passed, all going my way. Why get on them? They would only take me to people – friends, family – who wanted to make me better. Better, like them. Normal. Just living. If that's life, I don't want it.

The wet seeped into me. I moved because I had to.

Whom to get help from? In all this time, there was a dream that someone would rescue me. Someone would enfold me in soft warm arms; would kiss me and say: It's alright. It's alright. Someone would help me without wanting to change me.

Back through my mind I searched for that someone. I had been through all the constellation of family, friends, medicine men. One by one I had driven everybody away. I was now at last where I had thought I wanted to be: alone, absolutely alone. So utterly reduced that I forced myself to do something for myself.

Whom could I trust?

Alone in my parents' house, I picked up the phone. A friendly receptionist answered. "No, he's not available, he's in a therapy session at the moment. Can he call you back?"

I wanted to say no; hesitated; then left my number. I waited by the phone. The first time for years that I waited for something I wanted.

"Karen! How lovely to hear from you! It's been ages. I didn't get in touch because I thought you wanted to be alone."

Michael's voice was very warm. His words were wide open, full of feeling.

"I'm not very well," I said. "I need your help."

He was not surprised: our eleven-year friendship told him as much as his psychotherapy training.

He did not say: So you only phone me when you need help. His voice said: That's what friends are for.

We met at his office at the clinic. He did not say: God, how awful you look. What have you done to yourself? He listened gravely. He did not scold me because I had stopped psychotherapy – even though it was he who had recommended me to the therapist.

He did not play father or doctor. Like B. and Belkis, he accepted what I was; but unlike B. and Belkis, he was able to help because he was not too close.

Besides he had thought about help: really thought about it (that's his job). How to help without creating a debt. How to help by strengthening the helped person. He was not afraid to become too entangled because he knew the limit of the help he could give.

"I know someone who can help," Michael said. "He's one of my colleagues in family therapy. He'll phone you as soon as he can."

Why should this colleague be different from all other doctors? No reason: but I trusted he would, because he came from Michael. Michael had changed the definition of help. He was offering me the way out that I could take.

He didn't say: "Why did you never come to see me before?"

I could come only at the time when I could help myself.

6

MIGHTY MOUTH

My mouth always betrays
What my brain keeps well hid –
Even if I wrap a scarf around it.

MOUTH means mistrust. Mouthing words, making trouble. Mouth watering mania. Mouthfuls greedy grabbing needs. Mouth open man eating woman. Mother mouth, making babies. Out of the mouths of babes.

Shut your mouth: you're biting my breast – Mother. Shut your mouth: you're asking for trouble – Father.

I didn't hate my thighs – they were never fat. I didn't hate my breasts – they were always rather flat. My arms were long and slender, my feet neat.

I loathed my mouth, wanted to tear it from my face, pulled at it, abused it. Blamed it as the blatant cause of my misery. It was in bad taste.

My eyes could show suffering; but my mouth betrayed me by promising pleasure. It was the naked expression of my desire to bite on life. It seemed insatiable, incapable of satisfaction. It was responsible for failure with food, sex and psychology.

So I sewed it up, as I had read the mouths of compulsive eaters are stitched in hospitals. I left a tiny hole to let in caffeine and tobacco. I wrapped a scarf around it, yashmak style, and perused indignant accounts of female clitoridectomy in middle eastern lands.

My mouth had signalled sensuality for lovers, open smiling, crazy kissing. It felt to me of fear, man-devouring, killing flesh to eat meat. I closed it to them, shut my desire up.

67

TO EAT OR NOT TO EAT

I moulded my mouth into a thin line between starving and gorging, a taut wire between sanity and madness. To open it would widen the gap.

I shut the trap. Instead of biting on life, it bit me.

DREAM OCTOBER 1980

Went to a restaurant with the family. Food terrible. The restaurant was on several floors, and had narrow stairs. We ate, the food was very bad.

Suddenly, I felt the teeth on my upper left side loosening. As I chewed, they began to fall out and mingle with the food. I picked them out, there seemed no urgency in saving them.

We descended the stairs. As we passed other diners at the tables, I noticed that they were all eating desserts – sweet, sticky food coloured lurid purples and reds. They were finding the sweets impossible to eat, and at many tables there were plates left with barely-tasted desserts.

I began to drop the teeth and to scrabble furiously for them, trying to work out how many I'd lost.

I don't remember many dreams, though the psychotherapy seemed to bring some closer. Usually they were about food, in my sleeping fantasies I could eat it all, even if I did suffer disgust afterwards. To lose my teeth was a terrible punishment: I am proud of them, they are even, white and gleaming.

It was a just punishment, for if my mouth was too soft and vulnerable, my teeth were too sharp and terrifying. If men had hurt my delicate lips, it was only because of their fear of my voraciousness, that I would bite them, chew them, swallow them up and spit them out.

It did not take long before I became conscious that my hunger strike was a weapon against men. Refusing to eat with lovers showed that they couldn't satisfy me. It denied the possibility of sharing sensual experience. As I got thinner I gained satisfaction from proving visibly that they could not possess my flesh, and that I did not want theirs.

During the hunger strike I abandoned all my men friends and lovers. I abandoned the desire to have babies too.

Whereas women reacted with tenderness and compassion, men were mystified and bewildered. They wanted a woman, not a boy-girl in bed; they wanted a mother – not a Belsen baby. They felt obscurely to blame, and resented me for inducing guilt.

In the first hunger strike phase, I was at the end of a long, stormy affair with a man whose home I had formerly shared. He found it hard to forgive me for moving back with my twin; he had fought for me against my friends, my work, my writing. When I gradually gave them all up, he felt gratified; but when I shut off food and sex, too, he thought it had gone too far. He recognised the protest, and believed it was directed solely against him.

He loved to eat, and being sensitive about his weight, felt my self-denial of food as a clear criticism. The more he cajoled and threatened at mealtimes, the more tightly I closed my mouth. I recalled what a school-friend had told me when she was hospitalised for anorexia. The psychiatrist had said she was afraid of having a penis forced into her mouth. I felt afraid of having a whole man thrust down my throat.

He was an actor, always seeking a co-star. I wasn't quite beautiful enough, but I was a minor political starlet. When I stopped playing that part, retreated into my hunger striking self, he lost interest. Without the make up and footlights, there was only a plain woman, me. I showed it to him, and he rejected it.

Once I went to Edinburgh to see him act in a play. On the way back to London, we stopped at a motorway cafe. He urged me to eat: he had been away four weeks, and I was remarkably thinner since he left. I sat watching as he tucked into Forte's fare. He became enraged: "If you don't eat something, I'm going to smash your face in," he threatened. I was frightened all the way home, and left him in London feeling I was safer starving alone. I did not want to be force fed by a man.

When I gave up the first hunger strike, my sexual appetite returned in force. Food once more tasted delicious and sex seemed more sensual. I took life and love between my teeth without censure.

TO EAT OR NOT TO EAT

When I fell in love with a German man and went to live with him in Berlin, I wanted the child we conceived, and it appeared as further affirmation that I was living to the full, flowering, creative. But he did not choose fatherhood, and I could not force it on him. Against my own will, I had an abortion. Once again I felt powerless; once again I resorted to the weapon of the hunger strike.

We went to a pizzeria the day we parted. Outside, sitting in the Berlin spring sunshine I watched him eat while I toyed with a plate of vegetables. He said: "You have never given me the pleasure of enjoying food together."

I went back to London to a life of celibacy. I did not think about men or sex, they simply ceased to trouble my consciousness. I knew I did not want children, none could replace my lost baby.

There was my twin's lover, living in my flat; he said he wanted me, but I didn't want to be my twin again. Men felt foreign, alien.

At the magazine I was befriended by Mike, the sub-editor. He hated his job and kept the manuscript of a lurid novel he was writing in his desk bottom drawer, dreaming of better days. He was an ardent follower of the EST encounter therapy movement, and was always proselytising in the office, a joke to the journalists. But he was sensitive to my unhappiness, and tried to inspire me with the self-confidence his creed gave him.

He knew what a weak and wretched creature I was, saw how I agonised over my stories and wondered why I denied my competence. Sometimes he would persuade me to the pub, and I would usually beat him at darts. I preferred shooting the sharp arrows to talking useless words.

On his birthday, several staff took him for a drink, and I lingered, since he seemed to want company. He began talking about sex, saying that was my fear; I had only to fuck to overcome it. To fuck with him tonight, his birthday. "It could be the beginning of a new life," he promised.

I was shocked. Here was a man who only days before had spoken strong words against my hunger strike, had told me how everyone in the office was afraid I would collapse in the street, and that I should start eating immediately. I had felt scared at the attack, but had attributed it to the EST confrontation tactics. Now he was saying he wanted to make love with a body that would break to the touch. What could he want of me? What had I offered without even being aware of it? And how dare he assume I wanted him?

I offered a truce: I would eat with him. He held me to this promise, and we went some weeks later to a restaurant, where I ate dish after dish compulsively, greedily; then to a coffee bar for dessert. I had warned him my desire was uncontrollable, I proved it then. After that he left me alone and I ignored him.

Men mostly ignored me, accepting my asexual image. My anger against them evaporated as my contact with them diminished. People became sexually indistinguishable: they were all equally terrifying.

Some men did try to play feeding father. Maybe for them the hunger strike was a challenge, like reaching a mountain top or crossing an ocean; an unusual and difficult conquest.

Other men were definitely attracted to my boy-girl body. I called them Lolita lovers. They were invariably middle aged, usually divorced with teenage daughters of their own. Their social status prohibited approaching little girls in parks; they needed a presentable dinner companion, and I fitted their fantasies, being a professional woman of work and a physical spirit of innocence.

I had just given up my hunger strike, and was still painfully thin, when I met an American TV executive at a party. He invited me to dinner, and I accepted out of professional interest. We met at his club; waiting on the street for a taxi, he put his arm protectively around my waist, felt the bones and said, with pleasure: "My, but you're so skinny."

On the way to the restaurant, he told me about his divorce. His wife, he said, had never understood him. We had barely opened the menu when he invited me to spend the weekend in Paris. I replied that the acceptance of a dinner invitation did not imply the start of an affair. During dinner he told me that he had done his research, found out all about me and decided I was just his type.

Over coffee, he remarked: "You are so thin, I thought you were anorexic, but you can't be, you just ate." Of course anorexics eat (sometimes): if they didn't they would soon die.

As he walked me home, I struggled against his clumsy attempts to touch me. Every time he succeeded, he remarked with delight how thin I was. "Maybe a little too much, but you are irresistible." At my front door, I told him not to bother to ring.

I undressed, looking in the mirror. How could he find me attractive? What kind of distortions in his mind could reproduce me as the image of the woman he wanted? He was small and fat – was I his thin alter ego? Did he think I would prove he could get a model woman? A girl, fifteen years his junior, the desirable daughter? I found the idea repellent.

As I gained weight, I sought in men the image of the boy-girl I was losing in myself. They were younger men, who would affirm my womanhood. For the first time, I was struggling against being a child to the man, having rejected being the child of the family. I wanted once more a child for myself.

Still I felt trapped between sexual extremes. Was it possible to be something other than Lolita or the mother – something closer to myself? I answered the question by reading and writing, which I could do alone if necessary. Other needs seemed simple compared with the complexity of sex.

I can't say that I went on hunger strike to destroy my sexuality or to avoid a physical fear of men. I had enjoyed sex, it was the consequent emotional entanglement that had caused me pain. Being sexually neutral, physically inaccessible, was a welcome side-effect of the starvation. Through my isolation I had discovered the value of the space I created around me. Men threatened to invade it, to demand that I move according to their rhythm when I was just developing my own.

I have loved men, and will love more, but I cannot reconcile the images they create of women. I cannot be the goddess on the pedestal: I tried to become ethereal, but know I am bound to the earth. I would rather love a child of my own creation than be mother to a man. Sometimes I enjoy playing the harlot; but that can only be a passing fantasy.

I continue to see men afraid of the devouring female. Maybe that's why women politely take small bird-like mouthfuls when eating in public. If I showed my voracity, they would be bound to run away. My German lover gave me the tame name Mighty

MIIGHTY MOUTH

Mouse – I inwardly cursed my mighty mouth that would swallow everything if allowed to. "He wanted only the part of me that pleased him, that fitted his fantasies," I complained to the therapist. Who replied: isn't that what everyone wants from other people?

I pondered. Then argued: Yes, but he wanted only the least important parts. He ignored the real me inside.

So you could say I starved for love.

7

THE STARVING SELF

TO EAT ... OR NOT TO EAT?

THE DANISH pastry. It's large and round, wound in a spiral, with plump raisins nestling in the cracks. A smooth glazing of white sugar on the top, the raisins poking through, oven darkened, a little crunchy perhaps; a flaking of golden toasted almonds clinging to the sticky sugar. Sweet rich perfection, apotheosis of the confectioner's creation.

I saw the Danish pastry as I waited in the queue for my coffee. The coffee here is thick, dark, Italian. In its blackness I feel the promise of revival. It's different to the drippy, watery brew I drink all day at the office. Today I must have drunk ten cups... no, more: I've given up counting. I need it. Each new article, each phone call is an obstacle, a terror. It becomes harder each time to pick up the phone. I cannot move much; thank god for Daisy, who fills and refills my cup with coffee, keeps me going.

Roll a cigarette. Light it. Take a sip of coffee. My mouth tastes bad – nicotine and caffeine, nothing else for days. The bad taste fills my being. It's the taste of life: disgusting, sordid, inescapable. The other night, I said to my sister, I will never rid myself of this bad taste. I want to cut out my mouth. She could not understand. I tore at the sides of my lips, trying to convince her. I ripped my cheeks with my nails till scratches appeared. I had to cover them with make-up, but still people at work asked what I had done. I made excuses. I can still feel the stinging flesh.

The Danish pastry. Can't stop thinking about it. I saw some cream cakes there also; puffy eclairs bursting with cream. I can't understand why people choose the eclairs, they're a gastronomic cliché for self-indulgence. I saw a Florentine, too: a fine layer of sweet almonds, backed with dark chocolate, the colour of the

74

coffee; small specks of green angelica, a bright red glacé cherry in the centre. The angelica and the cherry put me off. They look artificial; so green, so red. Especially the cherry. It's almost indecent, like a great red nipple in the centre of a yellow-brown breast. Anyway, there's something insubstantial about the Florentine, it's too thin and delicate. Waferish, like my body. If I'm going to eat, I want something big and filling. The Danish pastry.

I need to feel the filling of my belly. Full to bursting. The only possible satisfaction from food: that fullness, to counteract and compensate for the emptiness I feel always. Feel? What do I feel? Numbness; except when I eat. Then I feel again. But what terror! What fear! I feel greed, insatiable, lustful greed. The overwhelming urgency to stuff myself full. The feeling takes hold of me, threatens to drown me. I can't stop.

Stop. Control. I can't control myself. No such word as can't, my mother says. No one can comprehend. When I take food in my hand, I shake. My heart races. I cannot breathe. Deep breath, try to take it slowly. Try to think about what I am doing. I am eating. I bite. Control slips. One tiny bite and I am lost, lost inside the moment of eating. I can't taste. I am not eating for taste, I am eating to fill a hole. But it stays empty, like the sieve that tries to drain the sea. An ocean of emptiness inside me.

Keep calm, I say to my heart; but it races heedless. Keep still, I tell my soul; but it slips away, beyond reach. The tiniest morsel, and I am lost, trapped in the torment of desire. I lose myself in my mouth, the biting, chewing greedy mouth. I am swallowed by my own stomach.

Control, I tell myself. I lose control. The merest taste of food triggers a treadmill of unconsciousness. I am compelled to eat until I can no longer stuff myself, compelled by some demanding demon inside me, that rears its head and bares its hideous teeth the moment I bring it to life by eating. It is only when I eat that I feel alive, feel passion and excitement, fear and loathing. Eating is the sole resurrection from the numbness that otherwise encloses me. And look what it brings! Lack of control. A horrifying, fearful enslavement. Slavering. I become an animal. I lose the dignity of humanity.

TO EAT OR NOT TO EAT

Eating is the only relief from the internal monologue eternal. Endless time is suspended. As in a trance, I race here and there with the speed of my pulsating heart. I am roused. These days, I can move only slowly, each step an agony. It is not only the physical weakness of starvation, though I cannot deny that. I move by inches because there is nowhere to go. Like a snail, I creep unwillingly to work. But when the mania is upon me, how fast I move! I run from shop to shop, buying things I don't even want to eat, feverishly biting on them, throwing them away after one mouthful, only to try something else. I feel the victim of some force stronger than myself, that moves me. I am driven, a vehicle out of control.

Suppress, suppress, I say to myself. Suppress the desire to eat. Walk along the street looking at my feet, so as not to see temptation. Suppress sensation, animation. Shrink my body, shrink myself to a skeleton. Bones cannot feel. Flesh betrays.

The Danish pastry. I can't get it out of my mind. What would happen if I succumbed to it? I wonder, how many calories? A lot – more than five hundred, probably. But that's a futile calculation. What difference could five hundred calories make, when I haven't eaten for a week? But if I ate it, my face would swell up; it always does when I eat. The betrayal by the flesh. People would say, you look much better. They would know I had eaten. I could not bear that, a secret discovered. Like when I lost my virginity, I was sure my mother could tell. Someone told me you could tell by the way a woman walked that she wasn't a virgin. I tried to walk as I had done before in innocence, but I couldn't remember how. People would know my secret. It's like that with eating. Not just the fear of losing control, but the fear of other people knowing.

I can't see the Danish pastry now: the counter is too far away. But I can remember it in every detail. Large and round, wound in a spiral. Like a snail shell. Yes, it's like a snail. And the toasted raisins sticking to the top are like those little slugs that sometimes attach to snails, plump little slugs. Before I got so thin, I felt like a slug, slow and fat. Slowly; I could eat the Danish pastry slowly, crumb by crumb, unwinding it, eating the raisins one by one, trying to savour the taste, to find fulfilment and satisfaction. But I

76

know it would not fill nor satisfy me. I couldn't stop there, I would have to go on. I cannot trust myself to know when to stop. I would be caught, unable to prevent myself. I would go hunting for the next thing, and the next and after that, more and more...

Then the self-disgust. No, I cannot eat it. It's disgusting. Like a slimy, glutinous snail, sticky, covered in stinking slugs. I don't even want to think about it.

Another cigarette. The coffee is cold. I've hardly touched it. It's bitter. That bad taste in my mouth. Wormwood. Gall.

Watching other people eat is safer. It gives a curious kind of satisfaction. At the corner table by the window, a man and woman are tucking into plates piled high. She is eating lasagne, forking thick layers of creamy white sauce and pasta and tomato coloured mincemeat into her mouth. It's steaming hot, I can smell it from here. He is slicing his veal slowly, ordering the food onto his fork with scientific precision: a sliver of veal, then a couple of mushrooms, then three green beans, then a slice of potato. Every forkful follows the same pattern. Odd how people play games with food. I wonder, does he know he is doing it? Every so often they pause to spear a tomato or a piece of lettuce from the shared salad bowl between them; or to take a sip of wine. They don't speak, the eating takes all their concentration. They are both fat, but they eat with obvious pleasure and unconcern. They look up at me, perhaps aware of my scrutiny. I lower my eyes to the newspaper in front of me. I don't want them to know they are under observation. I am a spy in the house of food.

At the next table, a group of Italian women are eating cream cakes. Layers of pastry with the rich cream between. One slices into the cake with her fork. The cream oozes from the edges. They laugh, they try each others' cakes, discuss the relative merits. They feel a little naughtiness knowing it's bad for their figures. But there's safety in numbers, they are consuming in company. They can share the illicit pleasure. I watched them choosing the cakes at the counter, taking ages to decide. Is it my memory, or some other's, that dredges up a scene with my child's face pressed to a cake shop window? Somebody, an adult saying: your eyes are too big for your stomach. The tristesse of being forced to choose only one cake, when others I had to leave behind might be more tasty. It is certainly my own experience, regretting my choice from the menu when I thought that others had chosen better. I always wanted to taste theirs too, to find out what I was missing.

I peer from behind my paper, pretending to read. I can't read it, there's nothing in it. The same news yesterday, today and tomorrow. Politics, gossip: only the names and dates are changed every day to give the illusion of keeping up with the times. Maybe it's just my jaded journalistic eye; in my state of obsession, nothing is important except the internal monologue. The newspaper is a shield to hide behind, so that I can watch others in the café consuming. If I stare too openly, they get nervous.

At the next table, a man is studying the paper with apparent interest, at the same time as eating a salad. He looks absent-minded about the food, as if it's incidental. How can he be so casual?

I can see also a young woman, her spaghetti topped with meatballs. She's looking around nonchalantly as she twists the long strings of pasta round her fork. She's slim and pretty, with thick black curls. Why doesn't she look afraid of getting fat as she eats?

The couple at the corner have licked their plates clean. The man returns to the counter for coffee. I watch him eye the cakes, have a momentary mental tussle. Then: why not? He picks up two plates – an eclair for himself, a cream slice for his wife. As he brings the tray over, I can see her face. Oh, you shouldn't have; mock horror, amused scolding. They eat the forbidden fruit with pleasure. It reminds me of another favourite haunt, the patisserie in Soho. There, the cakes are laid out on large plates on the tables. Customers choose which they want and pay later. I love to sit there nursing a black coffee, so close to these cakes – aficionados claim they are the best in London – and to feel myself resisting while I watch others succumb. Shall I? Shan't I? And oh! the pleasure of yielding, of pampering themselves.

How can these people eat in public with such abandon? Don't they feel shame at exhibiting their greed? I would not dare. Even if I could be sure of keeping control, I would not dare. Certainly not here. They know me here. The cashiers and the waiters know that I come here every evening after work, sit here for more than an hour while my coffee grows cold – and I never eat. If – just once – I were to destroy that picture, I could never return. I would feel shame, as if I had exposed myself.

Yes, there is something indecent about eating. The opening and closing of mouths; the munching and chewing, all these people around masticating like animals. Consumption. Admission of appetite, of bodily needs. It seems indecent, this constant exhibition of oral gratification.

It reminds me of that remarkable scene in the Buñuel movie, *Phantôme de la Liberté*. The dinner guests are gathered at table. You realise they are sitting, not on seats, but on toilet bowls. There is no food. One guest excuses himself, muttering apology. Around the corner, in a tiny closet, he hastily consumes some food, without enjoyment. He emerges, wiping all traces of the guilty act from his mouth. No need to get enmeshed further in the Freudian implications of oral and anal desires. Enough to recognise that food is for me taboo.

Black and bitter the cold coffee. A black headache takes shape behind my left temple. It's black with coffee and cigarette ash. Black with the black hole of my empty stomach. Time to go home, to sit on the bed and wait for sleep.

I walk out slowly. On the way, I take a last look at the Danish pastry. I can contemplate it now with equanimity. I am no longer afraid of temptation. If I succumbed, I would be like all those other people: enslaved by greed. But I'm different. They can see I am different. The man looks up from his newspaper. The pretty girl puts down her fork to stare. I'm not surprised. In the middle of the heatwave, while they are fanning their sweating faces, I'm wearing a thick woollen jumper. And even through its thickness, the bones of my back and shoulders are clearly visible.

HUNGER STRIKE

A Hungarian poet I know staged a hunger strike during his imprisonment in the 1970s for illegally circulating a book he had written. When he came to London, an admirer of his work asked curiously what the hunger strike had felt like? Had he suffered much? He had, after all, created something of a legend by its length and its laudable intentions.

"I enjoyed every minute of it," the poet said with relish. "I was imprisoned, a criminal according to the State; yet I was a celebrity, with people coming to the hospital every day for news of my condition, and the authorities begging me to stop causing them such embarrassment. I've never had such a fuss made of me since."

The admirer was somewhat disillusioned, but I saluted the poet for speaking the truth. Hunger strikers occupy an exalted place in our world: they appear noble, prepared to deny themselves nourishment unto death for the sake of an ideal. We are not supposed to suspect that they might enjoy it; that the action may serve their own needs.

I went on hunger strike also as a protest, the most effective I could mount from a position of powerlessness. My prison was social convention and the role I had created for myself, as a woman and as a worker. I had been an active feminist since my teens, and knew well the honourable antecedents: the Suffragettes early this century; the exiled Russian dissidents; the Irish political prisoners in British jails.

We who live in democracies are proud of our freedom to shout what we will; but that does not mean we are heard. I began by denying myself food as a form of self-control; I ended up on hunger strike because it seemed the only protest method open to me, once I had discovered the powerful effect of my starvation on others. It seemed to offer more than the shouting that is tolerated but unheard. And it is certainly less likely to alienate than bomb-throwing. As the Suffragettes and the Irish Republican Army learnt, a handful of hunger strikers draws more sympathy for the cause than any amount of violence against innocent citizens. Somehow, many people find it hard to bear the spectacle of self-torture even when they can justify state barbarity.

The hunger strike is so effective because you shift the guilt onto the helpless onlooker. At my most emaciated, what I saw in others' faces was the fear that I would die leaving my blood on their hands, a dreadful curse on their failure to help me.

At the same time as exerting this strong pressure on those around me, I could retain a sense of nobility. I did not have a clear cause, it is true; but I was employing the weapon of countless other good causes. I had chosen a difficult course, and was sticking to it with determination, against heavy odds, so I was at best to be admired, at least to be remarked on as unusual.

No wonder I found it hard to surrender this privileged position. No wonder many hunger strikers in state prisons persist unto death. To give in implies defeat, entails losing the elevated status you have gained with such struggle.

It is possible that many political hunger strikers carry on till they die without really meaning to. What begins as a threat against others can become a threat against yourself, which you are aware of, but find impossible to control. You become imprisoned in your own protest.

The ways out are often much harder than the way in to the strike. Take force feeding: I remember vividly the campaign in the early Seventies when the Irish Price sisters chose starvation in protest against their life sentences for terrorist bombing. We feminists could not defend their murderous aims; but we could cry out against the torture and humiliation of force feeding to which they were subjected. We re-enacted on the streets the horror of it: the tranquillising injection, followed by the insertion of a greased tube down the throat, and then the nauseous regurgitation of most of the foul liquid pumped into their resisting bellies. Doctors spoke out in shame against their colleagues who performed this torture; ministers shuffled uneasily when asked to defend it.

We on hunger strike who are labelled anorexic experience a similar revulsion at the thought of food being forced on us; and a similar reluctance to admit defeat by taking nourishment for ourselves.

Long after I wanted to say: I'm tired of it, I wish to abandon this self-torture, I persisted with the strike because there seemed no way out that could leave me my self-respect. I actually had to confront loss of self-esteem before I could say to myself: It is better to give up than to die.

But I could only admit that when I had found help from people who I felt understood my demands and would assist me to satisfy them. I could afford to surrender the self-esteem built up by hunger striking in exchange for a new self-respect born of recognition by others that I had real reasons for protest.

I must confess that the weapon appeals to me again from time to time. It was, after all, highly effective: it forced so many people to pay attention to my needs. Above all, it forced my family, especially my parents, to a crisis of confrontation that we may not have reached another way, and that I needed. It also forced me to change my life and my relations with others. In my self-created prison with its glass walls, I stripped myself to the bone, exposed everything I could – and it shocked those around into examining me and themselves, touching them deeper than any words.

The hunger striker stands above and beyond society. That's where I wanted to be; that's where the IRA prisoners, the Suffragettes and my Hungarian friend aimed for. Others might see me as physically handicapped by starvation; I saw myself as a heroine, the leading actress in a high drama.

I think we should respect the right of political and psychological prisoners to strike by starvation. If we say: Go ahead, It's a terrible way to die, but you choose it . . . , the weapon becomes blunted. During the family sessions, the therapist told me: If you wish to die, you have a right to, I cannot stop you. But then, don't ask me for help, because I don't deal in lost causes.

My parents were shocked, but he spoke honestly and truly. He was saying he wouldn't have my blood on his conscience. If I wanted to communicate with him, to express my demands, I had to find another way. He was refusing to enter my prison because he knew that was no way out, and besides, he likes winning.

I would not have responded, however, if I thought his only purpose was to coax me out of the protest. I could tell that he thought the protest worthwhile, it was only the means he was objecting to, saying it wasn't going to influence him, and so showing me the limitations of the strike.

I also knew that he differed from my friends, my family and the medicine men: he would not count it as a victory over me, or as a sign of my acquiescence to things I opposed, if I surrendered.

THE STARVING SELF

So I found that the hunger strike can only be ended if the striker sees the possibility of a truce with honour. The way out was to acknowledge my needs, to eat, to love, to live, without fearing the self-disgust of greed. The therapist won my respect, at first grudgingly; and since I could now see some value in another person, I could feel the value he found in me. Human diplomacy is the best response to the hunger strike.

FOOD AND FASTING

I keep to a strict diet, but I still sob whenever I see a potato chip.
– thin American heiress quoted in a women's magazine

Let's face it: in the fat Western world, most people admire the self-restraint of the skinny, envy the ability of others to refuse food temptation. Diet manuals sell as many copies as cookery books and everything is geared to encouraging the self-starver. So: many women remarked with compliments on my slight frame, wishing they had the control to emulate me.

I am convinced, nonetheless, that the desire to be thin for beauty's sake has little to do with the compulsion to starve. If it were the mainspring, every dieter would eventually become a skeleton; in fact, only a minority of women reaches that extreme.

I attributed my desire to starve rather to the need to control an insatiable appetite. Just as an alcoholic often has to force him or herself to steer clear of drink, I found it necessary to avoid food altogether, since even the tiniest morsel held potential for uncontrollable gorging. "The kitchen is a danger zone," I once remarked to my first psychotherapist.

To the rest of the world, you are simply getting thinner, the diet has got beyond a fad and has become a threat. Inside the process, I could discern the different phases, and see their importance. At first, the compliments (mainly from women) about my initial weight loss were pleasing, even though I had always been slim, below average weight.

What I began to enjoy was the growing concern of people around me.

TO EAT OR NOT TO EAT

Feeling empty, with nothing to offer, I now had my shrunken physical image as a presence, a talking point. I became the Thin Person; later The Skeleton, The Belsen Child. I began to need this image that others created to describe me. I found it hard to imagine myself any other way.

Along with this came a deep satisfaction at resisting food. I was superior to everyone else, to the material world that needed to eat and sleep and keep both feet on the ground. I could survive on my mind alone, fed by the fantasy of freeing myself from my body.

The feeling was real, not imaginary. Why else do mystics praise the exaltation of fasting? When you go without food, after a while you float on air. You are high without drugs, tripping on your own ability to transcend the earthly. In that state, it is so much easier to retreat inside yourself, to shut out the ugliness of human existence.

After the purification of long starvation, food can never have the same meaning, which is not to say that so-called anorexics can never recover. The reason I object to the current hospital cures, and the reason I avoided them so fiercely, is that they are based on imposing a normal eating pattern. The patient learns by rote when and how much to consume. It is not surprising that once outside the medical regime, or when the first crisis hits her afterwards, she returns to the former starvation pattern.

A learnt eating regime, like a calorie controlled diet, always carries the possibility of deviation. Small wonder that many people actually gain weight when they try to lose it, because they become too conscious of food, it rapidly evolves into an obsession. When imprisoned in the hunger strike, it seemed worthless to stop if the only alternative was to be rigidly organised eating for my lifetime. That was all the doctors seemed able to promise.

I had a different idea. I chose my hunger strike; so why not afterwards choose when and what to eat? I did not discuss it with anybody, for, mercifully, the therapist was not the least interested in weighing me or asking what I ate. (He did, though, remark once to my parents that I was a bit on the thin side for his taste – "But," he added, "Karen may disagree: as a German, I naturally prefer women a bit more buxom.")

Early in infancy we seem to lose the ability to satisfy most of our bodily needs according to our own rhythm. We work, eat and sleep to principles laid down by our social circumstances. I've never slept much, and revel in writing in the small hours, undisturbed by others' waking brain waves. I've always been fussy about some foods, but was never allowed to refuse them, out of politeness.

While I starved, I loved to watch others eat. I still enjoy cooking large meals for friends, though by the time they are served, I am often not hungry. I have become a sharp observer of other people's way of eating, and I find it increasingly odd that starvers should be singled out when everyone eats in a strange way. Mainly we think it is correct to follow the eating rules laid down by our mothers and by the school system; in practice, we cheat all the time. The Western model of three meals a day is a true norm – it does not exist, it is a statistical fiction.

Once starvation had taken me back to a kind of infancy, I started from that point to rebuild my sense of my own needs. I left the steady job, rearranged my life to develop another rhythm. It's not a possibility for everyone, and it may only be a temporary phase, or one necessary from time to time. I might sleep only in the afternoon; I can spend the whole day walking or listening to music. And I do eat oddly, though not in my own judgement. When I work, I cannot eat, feeling it slows me down and distracts me. There are moments when I relax and nibble constantly; days when I eat one meal and that's all. I never eat regularly three times a day.

Then I see how other people also create the problem. They wouldn't urge a book on you, force you to wear certain clothes to visit them; but they insist on your eating their food as and when they provide it. Refusal usually offends. Anthropologists tell us food is a primary means of communication; in choosing your own way to eat, you are asserting that you are different.

Most people keep their difference to themselves, otherwise they might be labelled as outsiders. I have found it easier to risk that and to make it clear what I will eat and what I reserve the right to refuse. It is also a tradition among Jews to reject the Gentile offer of pork, so I already had some experience of difference expressed through food.

There, I think, lies the connection between food, fasting and my fear of other people. I feel different, and felt afraid to show it in case I was interpreted as foreign and inferior. I feel greedy for life – not food – in a society that puts high value on self-restraint. I fasted to hide that fear of being judged, and in fasting placed myself beyond judgement while retaining my distinctiveness.

I don't sob when I see a potato chip: I eat it or refuse it, but contemplate it with pleasure. I may prefer eating peanuts in bed at five o'clock in the morning.

THE BOY-GIRL WOMAN

If self-starvation were only in the mind, people would not worry about it so much. It's that pitiful body, stripped of flesh, more naked than a new-born babe, which inspires horror and appears to plead for help. Living inside it is both pain and pleasure.

Regular dieters will recognise the initial satisfaction of weight loss, the triumph of taming the flesh, shaping the body beyond nature's intention. When others asked what I was trying to do by starvation, I would not reply, and they assumed it was merely a visible cry of anguish. But I had other goals.

I wanted to recreate myself in the image I held in my mind. My imagination saw me first trimmed in the physical being over which gravity held sway. I had felt heavy, sluggish, weighted by lassitude. Since I could not cut the millstone from my neck, I could at least remove the fat from my body.

The lightness I succeeded in gaining improved my feelings about myself. I had achieved something by and for myself in a world where I had no impact; I could prove the power of self-control, force others to pay attention, and at last come to terms with a body I had never fully accepted.

It is often said that women labelled anorexic want to return to the golden age before puberty. The typical loss of menstrual periods seems to confirm this – until we learn that the periods usually stop *before any discernible weight loss*, indicating other factors than starvation. Many of my friends have experienced loss of menstruation after a bad shock, when depressed, or for no explicable reason. The hunger striker does not starve deliberately in order to lose her ability to bear children, even if she fears motherhood.

For me, loss of periods was a relief because I could forget an inconvenient bodily function: it took me further towards the goal I was developing. There is nothing so potent a reminder of reality than the blood stains on your panties. I wanted to forget reality.

My image was not of the pre-pubescent girl; she is too unrefined, too earthy, longing for the curves of womanhood. Men with Lolita fantasies, and male poets in literature have created for us the picture of the slender, innocent young girl; I lived as such a creature, and I can remember well that my thoughts were of bicycles, coaxing silk-worm grubs to spin, and the doughnuts called koeksisters my Malaysian nanny made if I was good. I wrapped my mother's strapless bra around my flat chest, stuffed it with socks, looked in the mirror and wondered if I would ever grow such a sensual shape.

After losing enough weight to achieve fashion model proportions, I went further with the body-taming for another reason – to transcend sex, as my mind was transcending physical reality. My image was of the physical type I admire most, the combination of male and female that is called androgynous.

Some experts say the starving woman is trying to shape herself into the body of the boy that she failed to be born as. This is connected with the observation that many diagnosed anorexic have ideas and ambitions associated with sons rather than daughters.

If being a boy means having your own bicycle and not being told off for doing things girls shouldn't, I confess to wanting it at times. However, one of the benefits of growing up is that you learn women are superior despite their historical subjugation. Women's liberation was more profound for me than banner-waving or being part of a group. I took into myself the awareness that women are more interesting, more creative, more attractive and exist on a different and deeper level than men. I was proud of my womanhood, and would not have surrendered it to become a man.

On the other hand, I was also aware of a mental quality

described by others as male. When I wanted to, I could think in the way men try to: logically, holding my own in rational intellectual argument. I studied mathematics – not because I had a masculine mind – that taught me how men mould thought; and I enjoyed the mental gymnastics, it made me feel capable of reaching infinity.

I don't see my mind as split, rather as clearly combining the sexes; and when I sought to reform my body, I wanted to create the physical echo of that mental state. The boy element in my fantasy was very strong. I remarked that the male lovers I had found most physically appealing all had a boyish demeanour.

Among other people, I look more at the slim hips and tight bejeaned buttocks of young men than I do at the young girls who seem to me to be waiting for womanhood. When I looked at myself, hips slimmed to straightness, thighs trimmed to muscle, the mirror smiled with pleasure at my own double and dubious sexuality. I bought jeans in boys' shops and wore them with the softest chiffon or silk blouses.

As a woman, I could not be the boy Narcissus, so could not fall in love with my own reflection. Above the male/female divide, I could harmonise the beauty of both sexes. I became the ideal Greek boy, his image in the pool – and at the same time I was the shadowy sprite Echo whose love he captured.

Gradually I lost interest in my own reflection. Love cannot last if it remains passively looking. More and more I became the yearning spirit wanting to be rid altogether of my troublesome body. I wanted to free my mind from reminders of physical needs. I succeeded to some extent with food; but there were so many other bothersome duties the body demanded: hairwashing, bathing, clothing and undressing, walking and sitting. I felt happiest when I could lose myself in purely mental contemplation, playing word games with myself for hours on end; but I was always interrupted by the rude world.

When I spoke of death or suicide, I always meant the end of the flesh, never imagining that I would lose my mind. I spoke of emptiness, but I still had a strong sense of my own essence, the matter that cannot be lost or destroyed. I didn't spell it out for myself, but I desired a reincarnation in another form, not a rebirth into the uncomfortable world of the flesh. (I still believe I may be a cat, elegant female feline, in another existence.)

I kept hold of my mind when I abandoned the hunger strike, and it guided me through the body changes necessary to regain life. I was not able to contemplate my physical self, and I feared to be over conscious of it, in case it should again prevent me from recovering, weigh me down. I concentrated instead on an intense, almost bodiless sensuality, when to look at a flower or hear a symphony gave as much pleasure as touching or eating.

I now recognise the woman in me, welcome the monthly blood that binds me to my sex. But deep inside I am more aware of my androgyny as a definition of my being. I don't have to make the physical choice by forcing my body to accommodate to my mental fantasy; within my flesh I can exist as both boy and girl if my mind wills it. The control I exercised to starve myself can be reharnessed to shape life to my desires. The boundaries of human existence: age, sex, place, time, can only imprison if we accept their authority. It takes suffering to reach beyond them, but once we have tasted the rare air outside, it must be possible to stay there without the self-flagellation our man-created moral codes have always demanded.

Androgyny means having the best of both worlds, and that's greedy. Good. Eve is censured for eating of the tree of knowledge when God put it there in the first place. She is punished for her greed by eternal childbirth suffering. Should we not rather praise her for breaking the boundaries of understanding by finding out that good and evil are different? Should we not stop applying as a censure the term anorexic to the woman who tries to break boundaries to reach for the harmony of sexes within herself?

THE PERFECT PURITAN

By nature perhaps we would all be hedonists, if that awful puritan inside did not persist in criticising and preventing pleasure. Food starvation was only one aspect of my self-denial. I rejected all the pleasures of life and watched others partake of them with the scornful judgement of the puritan.

I embraced Hamlet's philosophy: How weary, flat, stale and unprofitable/Seem to me all the uses of this world!; and added to that his weary sigh: Words, words, words... which seemed particularly apt since I wrote thousands of words every day that seemed destined only to fill a space.

I did not even need to deny the distraction of films, television, company, music, books. I could not take them into myself anyway. I felt empty but nothing I consumed filled the whole.

Our society is anyway over-endowed with wealth too often stolen from elsewhere, so a certain revulsion may be predictable; but I renounced everything except warmth and a roof over my head. Paring my life down as I pared my body, I often wondered how other people filled their time, whether they really felt the enjoyment they professed at eating the consumer fruits. I searched for something deeper than the latest movie.

There's no harm, and I even see some good, in this kind of asceticism, provided it does not become a benchmark for judging others, and provided it is willingly adopted. I would not be a nun renouncing outside life, but I can see the appeal of the nunnery regime. I feel I have cleansed myself by fasting and retreat, though there are probably safer ways to do it.

Now I seem to see what the goals were, though at the time I could not define, only describe them. The mental and bodily will towards androgyny was accompanied by another aspect of perfectionism, the puritanism that caused me to deny pleasure. To admit I enjoyed anything would mar my perfection, would consign me back among the mortals with their feet on the ground.

I speak not of strength and superiority, though that is what I strove for, but of weakness and fear of temptation. I was so greedy: what would happen if I allowed my senses free rein? What Pandora's Box of wickedness would be opened up? Puritanism kept the lid firmly in place. I could not regain childish innocence, however hard I tried to forget knowledge, so instead I attempted to free myself from the guilt of consumption.

Isolation became ever more essential in case I betrayed that I was capable of enjoyment. I saw myself as the nun or the Ice

Maiden, chill to the touch and frozen inside. The cold that never left my bones was the only feeling I allowed myself. My last pleasure was masochism and its reflection in the pained faces of everyone around me.

Pity the perfect puritan, who imagines herself so far above her peers; she feels herself powerful but is trapped by self punishment. Accepting imperfection means being able to take pleasure in the tiny things, living in the pock-marked present, not the sanitised never-never.

ONE AND MANY

I have described my starving self as I experienced it, not one but many selves, each containing its mirror image. The dichotomies obsessed me and resulted in inertia since I could not resolve them any other way. Perhaps being a twin makes me more sensitised to the dual aspects of myself; at any rate, I can see this is what I have presented, a series of dilemmas in the shape of concentric circles with something at the centre I call my essence.

I cannot say I have created a whole out of these patterns. Yet I no longer feel the pain of being spliced. When I look in the mirror, I see a woman, not a thin body with a fat one behind jeering over her shoulder. When I make a protest, I want to act positively, not needing to strike by refusing food. Inside my womanhood, I can feel the boy and girl that I could not create by starvation. I satisfy the perfect puritan with the pleasure of hard work.

Doctors and friends told me that I feared the dark sides in myself; that I was concealing them because they were too frightening to face. Maybe they were speaking of my weakness, my fear of exposing vulnerability to other people. But I question how useful it is to speak of one factor, one significant episode, one aspect you want to conceal. What was hard for me was to find expression for my many selves against others' demands that you present a unity to them.

So I became one self, the starving self on hunger strike in the cell, which shut out the world without having to lose the connection with it. From that vantage point, freed of demands, I could view the outside, judge its value, look for myself without exposure and yet influence the constellation around me. At times I thanked the medicine men for setting me apart with their label.

I do not want to glorify starvation, since I took that route out of despair. My first instinct afterwards was to deny and forget it... then I recalled how I had tried to forget everything else and what poverty that had created in me. I said that I denied pleasure, but there is also a joy that comes out of wallowing in despair, and a satisfaction that emerges from suffering. In a perfect world we might know ourselves and not be driven to search; in this flawed existence we seem to need to swim oceans, climb mountain peaks, reach extremes to find the secret spaces in ourselves.

Anyway, I always achieved everything through conflict, otherwise it never seemed worthwhile. When the world appeared to offer no more challenges, I felt forced to manufacture them myself. Later I said to the therapist: I don't want to fight any more, I'm tired of battling when I could get what I want by easier means.

I felt it was the battles that had split me, the necessity to marshal my selves into the single suit of armour so as not to leave any unprotected areas. I was saying I did not want the old me, the old life back, it had led only to constriction and despair. I wanted to live and let live; to forgive and forget, like the Bible instructs us. It is indeed an easier - though apolitical - way to be.

He's sharp, that therapist: He's seen my kind before. He replied: Maybe you also needed those battles.

8
IMAGES OF ANOREXIA

THE PRINCESS AND THE POP STAR

WHEN Lady Di was announced as Prince Charles's bride to be, she was scarcely the perfect image of a princess, though the international press tried loyally to tell us so. The engagement photographs show a shy-looking young woman, with the well-built body and peaches and cream complexion that comes from generations of huntin', shootin', fishin' and eating the best country food.

The wedding preparations and grooming for future royal duties were naturally the subject of extensive press speculation. We were told that she had been ordered to lose a stone in weight to look better for the cameras on the big day. It was rumoured that, as befits a family of horse buyers, the Royals had demanded a gynaecological report on the future Queen to make sure she was capable of breeding.

The metamorphosis of Lady Di from an upper-class kindergarten teacher to a fairy princess was one of the most public and scrutinised cases of a girl growing up in modern history. With a world of potential fans far wider than any pop star or film star, she had to be carefully shaped to the part. She was destined to play the perfect woman: wife, mother and eventually Queen. She had to be the most successful media personality of our age.

I'm not at all in sympathy with royalty, but it does seem a lot to ask. In her twenty-first year, Lady Di became a wife, a princess and a mother. She also lost a lot of weight.

I had no doubt she was, like me, on hunger strike, when I saw a TV film of her visiting an old wrecked ship. I recognised the bones through her thick tailored coat; saw her hollow cheeks and distant eyes. She looked as I felt.

TO EAT OR NOT TO EAT

Some weeks later the more prying newspapers erupted with front page headlines that Princess Di was sick, suffering from "The slimmers' disease, anorexia nervosa". Gossip columnists hid their glee at this meaty morsel of news under cover of concern for the poor lady, who had clearly been pushed too far too fast. Psychologists, psychiatrists, doctors, agony aunties, opinionists and even leader writers had their say. A few ex-anorexics were trotted out to retail their case histories for the greedy audience that loves details of others' lives that they would not reveal about themselves.

Eventually the press dropped the subject in favour of an internecine wrangle about which paper was most guilty of invading the Royals' privacy. But by then anorexia was out in the open.

At the magazine where I was working, we took every daily and Sunday paper for press cuttings. "Look," the radio editor said one morning, "Princess Di's got the same thing as you. Good company you keep." And Daisy the photographer read every report avidly to find clues for helping me. I read them all too. I was fascinated by how the world views a famous hunger striker, and I was intrigued by the public image of anorexia.

The papers described it in detail as a dangerous, sometimes fatal malady. We were told, in the terms of popular psychology, that its victims were afraid to grow up; did not want sex; were too attached to their mother/father/thumbsucking/teddy bear to become adults and normal women. We were treated to vivid accounts of emaciation, malnourishment, and over-eating. And we were warned that this disease is reaching epidemic proportions.

Nobody could explain why. Hence the notion of slimmers' disease, and the growing criticism that putting too much pressure on young women to be slim had created this bizarre reaction. (This, from the newspapers and TV stations that earn their keep by first promoting foods to fatten you, and then advertising diet aids to make you thin.)

The more sophisticated papers and some women's magazines interviewed eminent anorexia experts who spoke of the family and its role in the illness. They almost invariably recommended a strict

94

hospital regime for cure.

Most of the Royal Family are on a diet; at any rate, with all those ceremonial banquets where they must eat, they are trained to be careful consumers of food. Yet none of the others seems obsessive about slimness. Why Di? Millions of women in Britain diet all the time, you can see by the profits of the diet aid companies, the sales of weight losing magazines. Most of them seem able to stop at some point, even though they rarely lose the weight they wanted to. Why did no newspapers ask the real questions about the so-called slimmers' disease?

I thought Princess Di was simply reacting to the image created of her, though I did not doubt she began by participating willingly in the creation. Once she had become the perfect princess, had produced a royal heir, what else was there left for her to do? Where could she discover herself? What was there behind the diamonds, silks and minks?

Around that time, too, a young girl pop star, Lena Zavarone, was being treated for the "slimmers' disease," the press told us, in a South London hospital. The papers invaded her privacy for the public interest of following her progress. They waylaid family members to ask whether Lena would ever sing again. She was an object lesson to every young girl: that stardom has its cost. She was paroled from the hospital for Christmas with her family; prying cameras captured her in the garden looking cold in a big coat and waiting, we were told, to eat a few morsels of festive fare with her folks.

I had to feel sorry for her, too. The hunger strike is a public expression of distress; but the striker is also trying to create space for herself, and these exposed figures must have felt even more vulnerable than I did. At least at night I could hide in my parents' house alone with my misery. They were being forced to remain within the image they were trying to reject.

The princess and the pop star are special - but there may be something they are trying to say to all of us. Look at me!, I'm a person, not the image of the woman you have created. Hunger striking seems particularly prevalent - or maybe just more evident - among the image professions: acting, ballet dancing, modelling... they are the fields in which the roles of women, not just how they look but how they live, are most clearly defined and most publicly in view. Some people in the public eye take to private drinking or drug-taking, but these, as women know, are destructive to work and to the appearance. Hunger striking is also eventually destructive; but there is the thin line, the tightrope one can walk between incapacity and continuing with the image. It is acceptable in these worlds for women to be very thin, as long as they maintain their functions, though there might be comment about the problem.

Lurid accounts of the suffering self-starver or compulsive eater do little to clarify why women do it, and how to resolve it. Pseudo-psychological interpretations are generally more satisfying to their proponents than they are to anyone inside the striker's constellation. Doctors recommending remedies in the mass media only give the medicine men more publicity and better status. Hunger striking is in danger of becoming fashionable through over-discussion unless people make a genuine attempt to understand what statement the hunger striker is making; and unless they become more aware that it is an intensely individual question, indeed, it is all about the woman as individual.

THE SPECTRE OF ETERNAL YOUTH

If the starvation was a protest against being forced to accept the role of a mature woman, it was also a sharp comment on the impossibility of being the ideal older female. Just as the princess and the pop star are held up for our adulation and emulation, so the eternally youthful film star is lauded, not for any talent, but simply for the ability to stay young. Especially if she works at it. The mass media are filled with details of how Jane Fonda, Joan Collins and other *grandes dames* of the modern Olympus keep their trim figures and fresh faces.

A salient feature of these new goddesses over forty is that they are, to a woman, obsessed with maintaining girlish slimness. They represent the unattainable, irresistible combination of womanly experience with the elasticity of youthful beauty. They demonstrate that we must refashion ourselves regularly, reshape our bodies to reappear renewed on the stage of life.

Suspended between menarche and menopause, I was able during the hunger strike temporarily to transcend age.

Wasting my flesh concealed the evidence of the years. The age of bones cannot be seen; the age of flesh is all too obvious. If I could deny the fleshly manifestations of middle age, perhaps I could also put to one side the narrowing options it represents for a woman.

(The reduction to a childish appearance was, however, mostly illusory. Though my body became more child-like, my face soon began to show the consequences of malnutrition. Dry skin produced new wrinkles; a moustache of fine dark hair developed over my upper lip – the textbooks told me it was anovulatory hirsutism. I began to look withered, as many women do after years of excessive dieting.)

I did manage, though, to bypass another crucial issue that confronts every mature woman: whether to have a child.

IMAGES OF ANOREXIA

There was no possibility that I could conceive, for the long starvation had clearly interrupted my gynaecological functions. For two years I did not menstruate at all. Often my mother would remind me that as an anorexic I was incapable of the natural womanly role of childbearing. I was afraid to be a mother, she implied. Perhaps that was true; at any rate, I was certainly afraid to reproduce my own mother in myself or in my relationship with a child. In refusing to be fertile, I was denying my mother the endorsement of the choices she had made. I took an unpleasant pleasure in telling her I did not care if I was sterile. I could not care for myself, so I could not imagine caring for a child.

When I was a teenager, I wanted to look like the glamorous ladies in fashion magazines. Somehow I never made it, and I forgot the ambition. During the hunger strike I removed all possibility of comparison with these legendary females, who raise the spectre of eternal youth. Now they seem to me to pose a sinister threat. To emulate them requires self-starvation. To reject them can inspire a hunger strike against the enforcement of a female image that most of us cannot achieve.

DRIVING OUT THE DEVIL

I could not identify with the princess, the pop star or the ageless goddess of screen and TV, however much I might understand the pressures that forced them to the extremity of hunger striking. They represented images of women that I had never sought to attain. When I looked for models for myself, I sought them invariably in literature.

The letters and biographies of writers and other artists taught me far more about the obsessions that plagued me than any number of clinical accounts of anorexia nervosa. Above all, I was astounded to discover that many, many artists have expressed their dissonance with the world, or the blocking of their creativity, by refusing to eat.

When Virginia Woolf wrote her impassioned plea for a woman writer to have a room of her own, she meant not only the physical space for quiet and fruitful work, but also the mental space and freedom to create. I would not argue that all women diagnosed as anorexic are potential Virginia Woolfs, but I do believe that everyone is possessed of creative power, and that hunger striking may be an expression of the very lack of a room of one's own that Virginia Woolf lamented.

(Here I find some support from the medical textbooks, which inform us that many female anorexics are ambitious, attempt to do creative work and have high ideals and standards for themselves and others.)

I found yet more rich food for thought in the letters and life story of Virginia Woolf. I discovered that she, too, had starved herself for long periods. Her biographer, Quentin Bell, describes it thus:

> She heard voices urging her to acts of folly; she believed that they came from over-eating and that she must starve herself.

IMAGES OF ANOREXIA

Leonard Woolf, her husband, wrote:

> It was extraordinarily difficult ever to get her to eat enough to keep her strong and well. Superficially I suppose it might have been said that she had a (quite unnecessary) fear of becoming fat; but there was something deeper than that, in the back of her mind or in the pit of her stomach a taboo against eating.

Fortunately, for literature, fortunately for us, Virginia did not live to have her genius starved out of her by medical force-feeding. She is remembered for her great works, not for her peculiar eating habits.

So what about the anonymous teenage girl labelled anorexic in the hospital? Does anybody – her teachers, her family, her doctors – think of her as anything else except anorexic? Do they imagine, do they say to her, that she could be something other? Or do they merely look at her label, at her emaciated body, and talk about how much she weighed last time and how much she should weigh next time and what she should eat to make sure that she achieves their definition of a satisfactory weight? If they do merely look at her label – and in my experience this is precisely what happens to a person labelled anorexic – they ignore her creative potential, her ability to break out of the food-or-not-food circle, by making something of and for herself and others. We are all born with creative gifts: even the girl sitting like a miserable bag of bones in a hospital bed.

The biographies of the great and famous have yet more to tell us about food, fantasies and starvation.

Virginia Woolf, we are told, was plagued by devils that she sought to starve out of herself. She was not alone. Lord Byron, king of the English romantic poets and courageous fighter for Greek liberation, suffered similarly. Contemporary accounts depict him alternately starving and gorging himself. He, too, wrote of starving out the devil.

The devil they feared was familiar to me. I wrote earlier that during my hunger strike, I felt myself to be a victim of some curse: a Belsen child, my aunt described me. I was the repository of all the

99

ancient griefs of my people, who were starved by the Nazis in the concentration camps. I was the scapegoat. And what is a scapegoat, but the incarnation of the devil (often portrayed with goats' horns): the devil who must be driven out and destroyed for the salvation of the rest.

The Jewish religion has its own devils. One, in particular, haunted me. It is the Dybbuk, who reappears so often in the Yiddish literature of Eastern Europe, where my family originated. The Dybbuk is a very special kind of demon. It haunts young girls. Yes: young girls, on the very threshold of sexual awakening – at the very age we are told anorexia nervosa is first exhibited. The Dybbuk causes these poor innocent creatures to go crazy. It possesses these young virgins, so that they strip naked, dance wildly and try to seduce God-fearing men. The Dybbuk has, of course, certain similarities with the serpent who insinuated himself to Eve, the first woman of all. The Dybbuk must be driven out, for he is contagion, drawing people away from God. The histories of the Jews in middle and east Europe are rich with accounts of ritual exorcism of the Dybbuk from girls who sometimes survive and sometimes die.

I wanted to be a good little girl. I wanted to please my parents, my teachers, my friends . . . but that awful devil, greed, would keep getting in the way. Because pleasing parents and others was so often in direct opposition to that other impulse: to experience everything, to grab hold of all the universe offers – to bite on life. I wanted food not only for bodily nourishment: I wanted to taste every possible taste. I wanted sex, not only for procreation: I wanted to sense every sexual sensation. I wanted to read, not only for knowledge, but to wallow in the words, to roll myself through a writer's phrases, to lose myself in careless abandon in the maze of fantasy created by another. I wanted to write, not empty words to fit in a space, but luxuriant rivers of prose bursting the banks of conventional form, or poems polished to perfection.

But how far this is from the good little girl! How far from the godly beings that are the ideal of the Judaeo-Christian canon! How far from the puritanical resisters of temptation!

And all the time, up above us, is a stern God who says: thou shalt not. Thou shalt not eat purely for the pleasure of eating. Thou shalt not fuck purely for the pleasure of fucking. Thou shalt not read purely for the pleasure of reading. Thou shalt not write purely for the pleasure of writing.... thou shalt not, thou shalt not.... thou shalt resist the devil that tempted Eve with that fateful apple (just one apple, I would say to myself, just one apple a day surely cannot do me any harm; but then, when I looked at the apple, I knew that to eat one apple, even the teeniest weeniest Cox's Orange Pippin, would open the floodgates, and I would be drowned for ever in the desire to eat until eternity...)

So I starved myself to starve out the devil; for only by denying the pleasures of life altogether could I hope to protect myself from temptation. I went away from temptation, into the wilderness, where there was no food, where there were no people... where prophets and saints and artists and other sinners had trod before me... in short, where there was no pleasure.

CREATION COMPULSION

SCHREIBEN:
My twin wrote to me
On the poster of Virginia Woolf
A publisher's promotion:
A Room of One's Own.

Sad portrait
Virginia almost virginal
In lacy mood
Premonition of self-destruction.

Command:
SCHREIBEN. To write.
I must –
I can't stop.
Compulsion of creation.

Unreleased, suppressed
I can't eat.
They call it anorexia.

Confined, constricted
I can't sleep.
They call it insomnia.

Moving like mercury
I can't stay still.
(Did I eat too much fish with
    quicksilver veins?).
They call it hypermania.

I call it
The I in me.